Roll away the Stone

Writings on the road to Easter

Brian Fahy

kevin mayhew

First published in Great Britain in 2014 by Kevin Mayhew Ltd
Buxhall, Stowmarket, Suffolk IP14 3BW
Tel: +44 (0) 1449 737978 Fax: +44 (0) 1449 737834
E-mail: info@kevinmayhew.com

www.kevinmayhew.com

ISBN 978 1 84867 740 1
Catalogue No. 1501455

Cover design by Rob Mortonson
© Images used under licence from Shutterstock Inc.
Edited by Nicki Copeland
Typeset by Richard Weaver

Printed and bound in Great Britain

Contents

About the author

Brian Fahy was born in 1947 of a Lancashire father and an Irish mother. For many years he was a priest in a Catholic preaching order, the Redemptorists. He met and married Maggie, and he has a son, Michael. Maggie died suddenly in 2012. Subsequently Brian wrote two books, *Finding Maggie*, which tells the story of his wife's illness and death, and *On the One Road*, telling the story of Brian's journey through religious life and into his own personal freedom. Both books are published by Kevin Mayhew. Brian continues to write homilies for Redemptorist Publications, and he has been a family mediator for twelve years, helping separating parents to make good arrangements for the care of their children. Brian is a lifelong supporter of Bolton Wanderers, and he has a lifelong love of the West of Ireland.

Introduction

I never liked Lent. As a boy growing up in the Catholic Church I always got the feeling that Lent had been invented to make us all miserable. Purple drapes and the absence of flowers, days of fasting and of giving up things: they all transpired to make my world bleak, bleak, bleak! Life is hard and you are not meant to enjoy it! This institutional dreariness did nothing for my soul. Just get through it!

Now I have written a book about the season, and I do not want the word 'Lent' to appear on the cover. It would still depress me! I much prefer 'Journey to Easter'. When the goal of all our striving is a bright one, when there is a joyful end to our pilgrimage, then the days of walking are lifted from being merely a trek and a trudge through the valley of darkness. We need bright purposes every day of our lives. We need to know that we are going somewhere. And the Christian journey that leads to a tomb also leads beyond it to the glory of Easter Day.

In writing this book I had to begin by reading the Gospel texts for each day of the season, and to my surprise I found in them nothing but positive intent, heart-warming encouragement and inspirational teaching. Starting from these Gospel words I have written a reflection for each day, bringing together stories and memories from my life, which I hope you will find positive, heart-warming and inspirational.

Our life truly is a journey from cradle to grave, and from the grave into the joys of heaven. It is, like all good pilgrimages, a journey that we make in company with one another. We have many tales to tell and good stories to share.

We need each other along the way for company, for cheering up on dark days, for mutual inspiration and support.

I offer you now my thoughts and my stories for the journey. Reading leads to reflection, and reflection leads to writing, and writing leads back to reading again. Sharing good stories shortens the road when it feels long, and lightens the heart when it is heavy. Most of all, as we walk along each day, we look forward to that great destination, our meeting with the Lord Jesus Christ himself, whose own journey began in a stable and led to a cross, and reached its glorious finale on that first Easter morning.

Brian Fahy

Ash Wednesday
Three easy pieces

Gospel: Matthew 6:1-6, 16-18

When you fast do not put on a gloomy look as the hypocrites do.

My father always looked very smart when he went out on a Sunday evening. He often wore his long mac with its neat belt, and on his head, in the style of those days – the 1950s – a trilby hat. When I see Roger Allam in the television series *Endeavour,* playing the part of Inspector Fred Thursday and looking very smart in mac and trilby, I remember my father. On Sunday evenings my father would make his way down the road to the Catholic Club 'for an hour', as he always said to my mother. Next morning, before I even woke up, my father, now dressed in completely different attire, would leave the house and catch the bus to Astley Green Colliery and to his work at the coalface. He was a miner.

He worked in the dark, deep in the bowels of the earth. Pithead baths were available by the time I was a child, in 1950s Lancashire, and so my father always came home clean. But I often saw other miners walking up the road from other pits, and their faces were as black as the coal they dug. The nearest I ever came to having a face like a miner was on Ash Wednesday, when the tradition of smearing our foreheads with black ash took place to mark the beginning of Lent.

My childhood memories of this season were never happy. The ashes got us off to a bad start – all doom and gloom, and 'Remember man that thou art dust and unto dust thou shalt return!' There was lots of purple around the church – a sign of mourning and misery – and to cap it all I was told that I had to 'give up something for Lent'. Sweets, or sugar in my tea. Why? Who benefits? It was all a downer and I just did not like it!

It still feels a bit solemn and sombre to me. Even after all these years I find it hard to shake off those early sensations. There is a feeling of religion having a go at life and trying to stop it; a narrowness of mind; a negativity about life. Lent is something to be got through, just as this life is something to be got through. And then I read the Gospel for today and I am stopped in my tracks. When I look more closely, I find that Lent is not a time for gloom and doom at all, but a time for smartening yourself up, a time to wash off the coal dust and to put on your good clothes. It is a time to be like my father on a Sunday evening, going down the road for good company and a quiet pint, and dressed for the occasion. Smarten up.

What does this Gospel say today? Well, it is Jesus telling his disciples how to live their lives in three easy pieces. Saying things in threes is a very common and popular way of communicating, and I notice that Pope Francis favours this style very much. Today Jesus takes three issues, the three main areas of our life – other people, God and myself – and tells us how to live them.

Other people – good deeds

The Golden Rule – a rule that most people recognise and see the value of – instructs us 'to do unto others as you would have them do unto you' (from Matthew 7:12). It is a simple rule of kindness and consideration, and we feel naturally inside ourselves that it is a good one. People are of the same flesh and blood. We discover that we belong to the same stock, the same human race, and what we feel in our hearts, minds and bodies, other people also feel. It is natural therefore to have this 'fellow feeling' for one another. And if we are in a good mood – if nothing has happened to hurt or upset us – we gladly try to follow this rule. But some days we wake up in a foul mood. Some days people say the wrong thing to us. Some days people do hurtful things and then the golden rule no longer applies; its goldenness fades away. Then anger, bad temper and acts of revenge are the name of the game. Our inability to cope with the negative side of life is our road to misery.

My father saw a lot of the negative side of life during the course of his journey through this world: From the injustice of poverty and unemployment to dishonesty in the workplace and public life, from warfare and useless slaughter to the breakdown of his own health. 'I'm not proud of everything I have done in my life,' he humbly confessed to his son one day over a pint, but he came by wisdom. One day when I was sitting beside him and sharing a pint, I made some observation about somebody being very difficult to deal with, and my father, as he lifted his glass for a sip, said to me, 'Ah, Brian, everybody has their troubles, but nobody has a right to be uncivil.'

Civility. This is the virtue of being fit and able to live with other people all the time. It is the virtue of treating them with honour and respect all the time because our human nature deserves honour and respect all the time. Now given that there is so much damage and difficulty in people, it is going to require a capacity for patience and suffering to be able to practise the golden rule all the time. There is no getting away from it. We are required to learn how to suffer one another. And every day of our lives will furnish us with many opportunities to learn!

The great thing is that in our human nature, in the way we are made, there is already a great capacity for self-sacrifice and love of others. Our nature, created in God's own image, is made for loving kindness, and every day we see and hear of great acts of goodness that people will do for one another.

A story has come my way recently that deserves to be shared with everyone. A woman by the name of Joanne Nodding, a schoolteacher, was attacked and raped some years ago. When her attacker was caught and had served his prison sentence, it was decided to try a process of restorative justice in order to help both victim and perpetrator come into a better place in their lives. This was five years after the attack, and the process would involve a meeting between the parties.

Joanne was surprised to see the look of fear in the eyes of the man who had attacked her. 'He was like a scared little boy,' Joanne said. She told him how the assault had affected her life, and the man started to cry. Joanne had been described in court by the judge as a victim whose life would be scarred forever, but Joanne did not want that to be the defining statement about her life. The meeting with her attacker worked wonders for both parties, and Joanne came away not a victim, but a survivor. Instead of being forever locked into the hurt and damage that was done, both parties moved from the darkness into the light of day.[1]

Living with one another is a huge task: sometimes a joy; often a sorrow. Jesus tells his disciples, in all their relationships with other people, not to do their good deeds for show, but because we are all children of the heavenly Father.

1. Carl O'Brien, *Irish Times*, Saturday 30 November 2013, 'I was a rape victim. Now I am a survivor.'

God our Father – prayer

Everyone loves a parade. In my childhood days in Lancashire, 'Walking Days' were a great tradition. Every church and chapel in the town – Catholic, Church of England, Methodist, Unitarian – all had their own 'Walking Day', and the local Tyldesley Prize Band would be out there on the road belting out tunes as we all walked in tidy procession with our banners unfurled, telling the rest of the town who we were.

Years later in Manchester during their traditional 'Whit Walk', the Catholic bishop had banned extravagances such as bands and statues from the procession and had tried to turn a tub-thumping Catholic march into a more reverential procession. But a little Italian parish in the middle of Manchester took no notice and kept up their tradition of two bands playing and lots of banners and statues. That's Italian culture for you!

Parades tend to be self-promoting institutions, and where rivalry exists the occasion for tension and violence is very near at hand.

Going to church on Sunday was always an occasion for dressing up in your best clothes. As a child I was never very keen on this and couldn't wait to get home to climb into my rough-and-ready clothes for playing out. Going to church on Sunday and walking in church parades are my childhood memories of public prayer, but in more recent times we have begun to see people in public roles pointing to the heavens and praying so that everyone can see them. Footballers seem to have developed a bad habit of doing this, clearly indicating that God is on their side and not on the other!

Jesus has the same lesson for us about prayer as he has about the matter of relating to others: don't do it for show.

Don't do it to look good. Do it because it is good to do. Do it because it is the most honest thing you will ever do in your life – to seek the face of the living God and speak with him. There is a special place for this encounter and it is not, in the first instance, the church building. It is the secret room of your own quiet heart. That is where you should go. That is where you will find the Lord waiting for you.

In creating each one of us, God has given us a heart, a sacred inner space, the centre of our being, our soul. This 'I', this mysterious person, born and growing with every passing day, is a holy place where the Lord God dwells with our own self. He never leaves this place. I often ignore him but he never leaves. Finding our way to our own heart is often the longest journey of all.

Finding our way to God is the same length of journey as finding our way to our truest self. It is a journey that seeks our truest freedom. It might well have been presumed in my own life, being a priest as I was for so many years, that I had come into a place of simple joy and happiness, but such was not the case. Having been encouraged into religion at too early an age, I never came into my own maturity of self until I had a breakdown. It was then that the journey into freedom began for me, and it involved leaving the priesthood to find my true self.

Today, in my secret room, my own heart and in the quiet of my own house, I sit with the word of God each day and ask the Lord to speak with me.

My own self – fasting

I ask myself the question: what is the purpose of fasting? The first answer that comes to my mind is the words of Jesus when he is fasting in the desert and the devil comes to test him: 'Man does not live on bread alone, but on every word that comes from the mouth of God' (Matthew 4:4). There is a good way to live life and a selfish way to live it, and we are inclined to be selfish. For that reason, a discipline of life is needed, a rule of life that will keep me healthy in body and soul and mind, and which will bring benefit to others. Fasting is part of the discipline of life. It teaches me not to put myself first all the time. It teaches me to regulate my life in healthy ways, and it calls to mind the suffering poor and hungry of this world and urges me to help them by sharing the good things I have.

When we are unhappy, our relationship with food is often the way in which we express our sadness. A most telling example can be seen in the life story of King Edward VII who, finding himself unappreciated by his mother, Queen Victoria, and indeed rejected by her as useless, found his comfort and consolation in food, drink and pleasure. A good man was lost somewhere inside all that carousing. Only at the moment of her death did Victoria open her arms and her heart to her son, and only then when he became king did the gentle and sociable soul of 'Bertie' – King Edward – appear.

Fridays, and especially Fridays in Lent, are days on which to remember the crucifixion of the Lord. They are a call to us to join together in community, as the Lord's followers, to deny ourselves food and to offer alms for the hungry millions of our world. When doing so, the good Lord tells us to look smart! Wash your face and comb your hair, the Lord says. Let the joy of your life shine out. Religion is no place for gloom. Sorrows, yes, and suffering too. But never gloom.

In the northern hemisphere we celebrate Lent in springtime, in the lengthening days when life is returning.

That is most fitting, for as I have now discovered in rereading the Gospel and in writing these words, Lent is the season for the renewal of life, not for its denying.

> 'God, create a clean heart in me, put into me a new and constant spirit.' (Psalm 51:10)

Thursday after Ash Wednesday
Carrying a cross

Gospel: Luke 9:22-25

> *If anybody wants to be a follower of mine, let him renounce himself and take up his cross every day and follow me.*

In 1964 an old Redemptorist priest died. His name was William Locke. Among his belongings was the mission cross that he had used all his life whenever he climbed into a pulpit to preach. It was a simple wooden cross with the figure of Jesus crucified upon it, and its size made it comfortable enough to fit into the black belt on the Redemptorist habit. By tradition, when an old priest died, his cross would be taken and passed on to the next new recruit who came along to join this missionary order of preachers. That new recruit in the autumn of 1964 happened to be myself. The cross was given to me as I began my first year of training and it has been with me ever since, for 50 years. When I left the priesthood and the Redemptorists, I left behind all the trappings of that life – habit, rosary beads, clerical dress – but I found that I could not or did not want to part company with the cross. It had been my companion for so long, and I was not walking away from the cross of Christ. So the cross came with me and I have it still; it is here beside me as I write these words.

In today's passage Jesus tells his friends that the cross is part of our life, every day we live. Jesus himself will suffer grievously, and we, too, must learn to carry the cross. What does this mean? Let us ask Saint Paul. When Saul of Tarsus came to hear about this crucified Jesus and his followers, he was determined to stamp out this upstart religion. He was full of fire for justice and for the tradition of his forefathers. This crucified Lord was, to Saul, plain nonsense. Then he met the crucified and risen Lord on the road to Damascus and his world turned upside down. He had to re-figure everything. Saul was a clever man, very intelligent and full of energy. Now he became Paul, and he turned all his energies to preaching Jesus Christ.

At one point, in Athens, Paul tried to use his cleverness, his intelligence, to explain the 'Way of Christ' to his audience, and they laughed at him. The experience was chastening, and Paul learned powerfully from it. No more would he try to preach Jesus in terms of human philosophy and speculation. Instead he realised that the only thing he really knew about Jesus was that he endured the cross and was restored to life. Human intelligence does not know what to make of that, but divine intelligence does. Understanding life takes more than our minds can grasp. There is an intelligence of the heart, a path that leads through suffering into a greater light.

So I ask again, what does it mean 'to carry the cross'? It means to persevere in love through all our sufferings. The cross is the expression of persevering love. The cross is the great sign of love, a sign that someone would endure all that wickedness can do, and persevere in love for us. It is suffering love that redeems the world. Christ on the cross, the horrendous sight of goodness defeated, becomes Christ the lover of humankind, whose death is not the end but only a prelude to the life of resurrection.

A hundred years ago, young men in their thousands went off to fight a war and died in the muddy fields of Flanders and other theatres of battle. They were so young to lose their lives. A whole generation was destroyed: so many lost lives; so many broken hearts. In the midst of so much madness and so much waste, the cross of Christ stands as emblem of sorrow and hope of glory. The wickedness that took such young lives away is countered by the one who hung on a cross and who promised, 'Today you will be with me in paradise' (Luke 23:43).

One of those young soldiers, an Irishman by the name of Tom Kettle, found himself in the middle of a war whose motives, many of them, did not make sense to him. His own desire to see an independent Ireland flourishing within the British Empire and within a friendly Europe took a hammering when the Easter Rising broke out in Dublin. He went back to Flanders, a loyal Irishman fighting in the British Army, having to rethink his purposes and their meaning. From the trenches he wrote a letter/poem to his young daughter in 1916, to try and explain to her how he came to die and not return to her, should that happen. How many men like him died in a foreign field, leaving behind the ones they loved most in this world!

To my daughter Betty, the gift of God

In wiser days, my darling rosebud, blown
to beauty proud as was your mother's prime,
in that desired, delayed, incredible time,
you'll ask why I abandoned you, my own,
and the dear heart that was your baby throne,
to dice with death. And oh! They'll give you rhyme
and reason: some will call the thing sublime,

and some decry it with a knowing tone.
So here, while the mad guns curse overhead,
and tired men sigh with mud for couch and floor,
know that we fools, now with the foolish dead,
died not for flag, nor King, nor emperor,
but for a dream, born in a herdsman's shed,
and for the secret Scripture of the poor.

A few days later Tom Kettle died.

The dream born in a herdsman's shed is the life of Christ, and the cross of Christ. Having received my own crucifix all those years ago, it is my turn now to pass on to whoever may read this my belief in the cross of Jesus. The Way of the Cross is the pathway of love that perseveres through suffering unto the morn of Easter and resurrection.

> 'Yahweh takes care of the way the virtuous go, but the way of the wicked is doomed.' (Psalm 1:6)

Friday after Ash Wednesday
Seasons of the heart

Gospel: Matthew 9:14-15

The time will come for the bridegroom to be taken away from them, and then they will fast.

I was born in January 1947. It was a very harsh winter. I have seen old newsreel film of cold, grey skies and deep snow, and steam trains trying to maintain services through blizzard conditions. I have no recollection of these things, but my mother told me that one day she looked into my cot and could not find me, and then she rummaged about and discovered that I had made my way, under the blankets, to the very bottom of my cot, presumably to keep warm!

The first really cold winter I remember came in 1963 when I was 16. I was away from home, in a junior training college for priests, and the snow was so bad we could not get out or move very far for weeks on end. The priests in charge devised special gym classes for us just to use our energies. It was a grim time. Winter can be very beautiful on the eye, with frost on branches and robins hopping about, but the cold and the dark skies can be very depressing.

The seasons of the soul are very much like the weather – sunny days and cloudy days, changeable moods and even storms. It is the peculiar challenge of teenage years to be changeable, to be very much the victim of our moods. The achievement of maturity is to master our moods and to live with a more settled soul. But sorrow and sadness cannot be avoided completely. Dark days will visit us and often take us by surprise.

The most common form of sorrow that we meet is grieving, sadness of heart at the loss of a loved one. On one occasion, when I was a young priest on a parish mission, I was instructed by my senior colleague to preach a sermon on 'Death'. I remember getting up to speak and telling the assembled congregation that I had no personal experience of losing anyone close to me at all. I am sure the people in the pews that day could have preached a better sermon than I!

Since that time, of course, many experiences have come my way, and in a sermon I now would be able to call on a number of experiences of loss. Life is our great teacher. There are experiences of grief that come through death, and others that come through the ending of a relationship – through separation and divorce especially.

For the disciples of Jesus, grief comes to them in the most shattering form of all. Their master is arrested, tortured, condemned and led out to a cruel death. Their reaction is, after an initial skirmish with a sword, to run and hide and escape the coming violence, like any of us would.

Whenever we read the gospel story we come across instances where Jesus speaks about his coming suffering. Each time the disciples do not understand what he is talking about. When they do begin to grasp what Jesus is saying, Peter responds by refusing to accept such a prospect. It is all very natural. None of us likes to be told sad things or to contemplate a gloomy future.

In the days of Jesus' active life, when the disciples are on their travels with him about the Galilean countryside, it is all sunshine and wonderment that they feel and experience. These are happy days. They are not days for fasting or for sorrow, and so when some disciples of John the Baptist quiz Jesus about his lack of religious fasting, Jesus explains himself to them. He is the bridegroom and these are days of wedding joy. It would make no sense to fast now. But, yes, the days will come . . .

In this season of Lent, a season that leads us on a journey to Jerusalem where Jesus will be handed over to his enemies, our eyes will travel to the cross of Calvary and the crucifixion of Jesus. That day was the darkest day of all. Saint John the Evangelist, looking back in old age and remembering the day he stood at the foot of the cross with Mary, the mother of Jesus, talks about Jesus being 'lifted up' (John 12:32). The first lifting up was painful to see, but the more John looked, the more he saw that this lifting up was an exaltation, a climbing to great height, a glory of love triumphant over all wickedness, and even over death itself.

This is the way we now look on all our sorrows. We look to the cross of Jesus, and we know that our suffering will pass and that our joy shall return.

My own most painful sorrow has been in losing my beloved wife, Margaret, to a sudden death. But to my utter amazement and gratitude, I have made a journey through grief that has brought me into a place of serenity. I have been surprised by the way that life, and love of life, has returned to my soul.

I would say that the hardest suffering I have ever experienced was nothing to do with the grief I have felt over my wife. Rather it was the feeling of life having passed me by when, still a priest, I felt no joy in the life I was trying to live. This I think is the greatest suffering that people actually suffer: not being free to live the life they want to live.

When people suffer any form of oppression, especially when they have been victims of abuse, and those experiences and memories burden their lives each day, that is a suffering of evil from which all need to be rescued. To suffer sadness and sorrow over loss is normal and comes to us all. To suffer because of wickedness done to us, that is the great enormity and we must try, in Christ Jesus, to help free people who are in such suffering and pain.

> 'Have mercy on me, O God, in your goodness.' (Psalm 51:1)

Saturday after Ash Wednesday
Sinners all

Gospel: Luke 5:27-32

> *[Jesus] noticed a tax collector, Levi by name, sitting by the customs house, and said to him, 'Follow me'.*

On 19 August 2013 in the Casa Santa Marta in Rome, Pope Francis gave an interview to a Jesuit magazine, conducted with Father Antonio Spadaro. The very first question he was asked was about his own personal self, the man born Jorge Bergoglio: 'Who is Jorge Mario Bergoglio?' The Pope sat in silence for a while. It was such a simple, straightforward question, and yet such a deep one. How do you begin to say who you are? The interviewer speaks again, this time to ask if it is all right to ask such a question. Pope Francis nods his head. He is thinking, as any of us would if suddenly landed with such an opening inquiry. Then the Holy Father begins to reply: 'I do not know what might be the most fitting description . . . I am a sinner. This is the most accurate definition. It is not a figure of speech, a literary genre. I am a sinner.'

Now that he is launched into his answer, Pope Francis begins to sail out into a fuller response. 'I am astute,' he says, 'I can adapt, but I am also a bit naïve, but the deepest thing, the truest thing is to say I am a sinner.' It is then that Francis turns his mind to Saint Matthew, the tax collector. His motto on becoming a bishop was taken from some words uttered by Bede the Venerable who said of the calling of Matthew that Jesus looked upon him with feelings of compassion and love and chose him to be a follower. In the same way, Pope Francis felt that Jesus looked upon him with feelings of compassion for a sinner and chose him to follow him. Whenever the Pope gazes at the painting by Caravaggio, *The Calling of Matthew*, he says he feels very much like the tax collector with his hands still holding on to his money; a sinner whom the Lord has looked upon.

To be a sinner is to be one among equals in this world, for we are all sinners. This is not to damn ourselves but is rather to be realistic about our desire for goodness and our inability to achieve it by ourselves. In saying this, in admitting this, we make a level playing field of the whole world and of all human beings. We are all the same. And yet, it is clear as well that we are not all the same. There are many differences between us in this world, and we have devised many ways of marking out these differences. In a famous television sketch many years ago, John Cleese, Ronnie Barker and Ronnie Corbett acted out those differences between upper class, middle class and lower class, between those who look up to people and those who look down on people, and those at the bottom who know their place!

The divisions that we make between people in society have enormous effects on our lives, in terms of money, status and equality before the law. We tend to be more deferential around the well-to-do and the well spoken, and a lot more casual around the poor and the underprivileged. Saint James, in his letter to all Christians, reminds us of this natural bias and weakness in our nature (see James 2:1-9). The Pharisees of Jesus' time were absolutely scandalised that he would think to associate with the lower orders, and they lost no time in telling him so. The answer Jesus gave them leaves us

– and them – in no doubt about the human race: 'I have not come to call the virtuous, but sinners to repentance' (Luke 5:32). We are sinners – all of us. There are no perfect specimens here!

The meeting of Jesus with Levi/Matthew is powerful. At the heart of this encounter is the grace of 'acceptance'. This was the one thing lacking in the life of the tax gatherer. He had steady employment and good money, but as an employee of the Romans he found himself despised by his own people as a turncoat. Without acceptance among our fellow human beings, our life is not worth very much. There can be no flourishing of the spirit, no simple joy. And money will never compensate. Now, in meeting Jesus and hearing the words 'Follow me', Matthew is newly born.

The new follower throws a party and lots of his friends turn up, not just for the free beer, but because the action of Jesus for one of their number speaks volumes to them all. They all feel a sense of acceptance by this wandering preacher, and they want to celebrate that.

In public society a line is often drawn between who is and who is not acceptable. Not long ago, unmarried mothers were considered unacceptable and a scandal to be hushed up. In royal society, a physical illness or deformity was often considered shameful and was kept hidden from the public eye. Kaiser Wilhelm of Germany and his 'useless' arm is an example. John, the son of George V, is another. This boy's epilepsy caused him to be kept hidden from public view. The inability of Queen Victoria to accept her son 'Bertie' just as he was put a blight on that man's life for the rest of his days.

In this matter of acceptance, we all hold a power over the lives of others. If there are people in our own life whom we refuse to accept or to forgive, or to tolerate, then we are exerting a power of darkness over them. Where we have been offended, it is for us to pray that the Lord will grant us the grace to forgive. We are all sinners in need of repentance, and the Lord calls us all to follow him.

'You are my God, take pity on me, Lord.' (Psalm 86:2-3)

FIRST WEEK OF LENT

First Sunday of Lent

Testing

Gospel: Mark 1:12-15

The Spirit drove [Jesus] out into the wilderness and he remained there for forty days, and was tempted by Satan.

A storm is brewing. Weather warnings are being given. Strong winds, some as strong as 100 miles an hour, are expected, along with driving rain followed by snow showers. Flooding is likely, as is great disruption to traffic and travel. It is good to be at home indoors at such times, and not to be out in that weather, exposed to those fierce elements. Nature is a raw force and needs to be respected. News of the storm reminds me of the way sailors talk about the sea. They love to be at sea, but they never take her for granted. She can show dangerously stormy moods and deserves great respect from us mere humans.

As it is with the physical world, so it is with the human and spiritual world. Storms of destruction come upon us when people become enraged and threatening, when angry moods and violent words are hurled at one another, when nations choose to go to war and all hell is let loose for soldiers and civilians alike. The bombings of cities in World War II and in more recent times are as fearful as the storms that come in hurricane and tornado to devastate the land.

War and peace; calm and storm; the battle of good and evil. Such is the dramatic scene that Mark puts before us at the beginning of his Gospel, when he tells us that the Spirit drives Jesus out into the wilderness, to be there for 40 days among the wild beasts and to be tempted by Satan. It is a great contest. Mark tells us no more than this, whereas Matthew and Luke give us the drama of the three temptations and their rebuttal by Jesus. Yet, in their brevity, Mark's words express forcefully the drama of human life. 'He who is not with me is against me; and he does not gather with me, scatters' (Luke 11:23). There is no sitting on any fence in this story. Either you are for goodness in all its forms or you are corrupt. Which is it to be?

Jesus was on his own in the wilderness for 40 days. It is quite a challenge to be by yourself for any length of time. There are no distractions. You are thrown back upon yourself. You must eventually face yourself and see if you can live with the person you find there. It is a time for discovering things about yourself that you never knew, because you never looked before. It is a time for honesty. You cannot kid yourself forever.

Some years ago a few men went into a monastery for a week, to try the life of silence. At first they could not cope with it. They became quickly bored and looked for escape. Then, as they grappled with their moods and their impatience, they began to enter into the silent world of their own interiority and to appreciate the blessings their silent days were giving them. Towards the end of their time there they had become very jealous of their silence and did not want to lose it. They had gone into the wilderness and fought with their own demons, with their accuser, Satan, and had emerged better and wiser men. Indeed, they were transformed by their desert experience.

In our own lives, in our own homes, it is possible for us, especially if we live alone, to create a silent space for ourselves. We can turn off the television and the radio and the music. We can sit still. We can go for a walk. We can find our own wilderness that is free from distraction; we can make our own monastery of peaceful quiet. We can sit with the word of God and invite the Lord to speak with us.

It is in this environment that wisdom comes to us, and calmness of soul, and considered reflection: qualities much needed in our fast-moving world. We live in a world of constant chatter, constant talking, and constant argumentation. Who listens? Who is silent to hear? Very few, it would seem. But why not you? Why not me?

In his life on Earth, Jesus would go up into the hills regularly to be quiet and still and to be with his heavenly Father. Out of this deep silence his wisdom came. All his learning, all his teaching in the Sermon on the Mount, all his wonderful parables poured out of the richness of his heart, nourished in silent prayer with his Father. What Jesus learned at his mother's knee, at his father's side, what he learned in school and synagogue, and in the rough and tumble of the streets and alleyways of Nazareth, all came together in the silence of his soul when he sat among the Galilean hills to contemplate it all.

From his prayer life, Jesus also gained the strength of character to stand his ground in this world, to face his opponents and to deal calmly with moments of confrontation. This is true strength indeed – to be able to remain calm and considered when being provoked and attacked. The pages of the Gospels are full of encounters where Jesus has to respond to awkward people and their awkward questions. It is his desert struggle with Satan, his desert struggle with himself even, where issues of patience and wanting our own way are challenged by our basic helplessness, by our own fragility as creatures, that equips Jesus for the fight; this and his prayer union with God the Father that equips him for just such dramatic episodes.

And therein lies the lesson for our own lives. Quiet, reflective time, time away from other distractions, prayerful time will give to us wisdom for our daily lives, and courage and confidence in our daily encounters to be ourselves and to meet opposition with a good grace.

> 'Yahweh, teach me your way, how to walk beside you faithfully.' (Psalm 86:11)

First Monday of Lent

A simple reckoning

Gospel: Matthew 25:31-46

I was hungry and you gave me food.

Archbishop Anthony Bloom, a Russian Orthodox priest, was born into wealth and affluence. His father worked for the Russian diplomatic service and was stationed in Lausanne in Switzerland when Anthony was born in 1914. Soon afterwards the family were posted to Persia, and that is where they were when the Russian Revolution broke out in 1917. The family escaped to Paris, which is where Anthony grew up. He trained to be a doctor, and worked in hospitals in Paris during the Second World War. By this time he had also found his faith in God, and he trained to be an Orthodox priest.

As he looked back at his early history, Archbishop Anthony told how the first Jesus he came to know resided in splendid churches and cathedrals, surrounded by rich adorning and magnificence. Then, during his experience of being a refugee and an immigrant, he found a second Jesus – a Jesus who lived in humble dwellings where people gathered for their prayers; a Jesus who lived among the poor. He discovered the real Jesus, the Jesus who happily called himself a 'Son of Man', who was one of us, the Lord in flesh and blood.

The Lord Jesus, whom the Creed calls 'true God and true man', came among us in our nature, and it is in this everyday human nature that we will find him.

Today Jesus tells us the story of the Final Judgement, the day when God will hold the reckoning with all humankind. This is the day for truth. This is the day for justice.

Jesus begins the story with a grand opening. The Son of Man will come in his glory, and he will be escorted by all the angels, and he will take his seat on his throne of glory. This is very impressive. This is the big deal. All of humankind will be assembled before him and a great dividing will taking place – of the good and the bad. And then comes the great surprise and shock.

Jesus does not talk about churches or cathedrals or saying prayers, or even about being religious. Jesus begins to talk about ordinary everyday things, human interactions and human relationships. He speaks to us about ordinary acts of kindness and care that we might do, one for another. And the list is interesting.

To give food and drink – to give welcome to the stranger – to clothe and shelter the poor and needy – to visit those who are sick – to visit and care for those whose lives have gone wrong. This list covers every area of our life where we stand in need of help from one another. This is our social condition and our social duty. The issues are poverty, displaced persons, shelter, illness, wrongdoing and hard times. None of us lives our life without the help of others, and we are not meant to do so.

In the world, however, things are different. We regard wealth and prosperity as a desirable goal for our personal lives. We like to wine and dine. We like to travel. We feel pressurised by the problems that other people have – poverty, homelessness, prison records – and we like to keep these problems at a safe distance. Certainly we need some law and order to protect us from being inundated by the social issues of the day. We tend to divide the world into the haves and the have-nots, into those who can survive and those who cannot. And like the Pharisees of old, we like to keep the lower orders well away from our comfortable lives. Some people are just hopeless cases, and that's all there is to it.

This poor way of looking at things is named and shamed by Jesus when he tells his story of the Judgement. 'When did we see you hungry or thirsty? When did we see you sick or in prison and not help you?' people ask. Jesus is not slow to reply: 'In so far as you neglected to do this to one of the least of these, you neglected to do it to me' (Matthew 25:45). It is our selective blindness that is our problem.

Sometimes, as we listen to this story, and especially as we listen to earnest sermons based on it, we can feel depressed at the very prospect of trying to live a holy life. Moral earnestness and constant do-gooding simply makes us weary, and the sheer amount of injustice and wrongdoing in the world can halt us even before we begin.

It is here that Archbishop Anthony may be of help to us. In his book, *Meditations on a Theme*, he says that Lent, and any time of spiritual endeavour, is a time of joy because it is a time for coming home, a time for returning to the simple things of life, a period when we can come back to life.[2] The notion of joy, coupled with strenuous effort, with ascetical endeavour, with struggle indeed, runs through the whole of our spiritual life, because the kingdom of God is to be *conquered.* It is not something that is simply given to those who lazily wait for it to come along.

The challenge that Jesus puts before us in his story of the Last Judgement concerns the simple facts of everyday life. It is a joy for us to be kind and to share all we have. It is a joy to be able to help others every day. It is a joy to bring comfort to those who are sick, and to have a care for those whose lives have gone astray.

---

2. Anthony Bloom, *Meditations on a Theme*, Mowbray Publishing, London and Oxford 1973.

Archbishop Anthony says that Lent is a time for coming home. Here at home each day I need food and drink and, thank God, I am fit enough to go to the shops, where these things are provided. I need clothes and shelter and, thanks be to God, I have these things about me. I have friends and family with whom I am in constant touch. I am in good health, thank God. I have not gone astray.

All these things are shared blessings, and one day I may need more help with some or all of them – the simple bare necessities of life.

'The words I have spoken to you are spirit and they are life.' (John 6:63)

First Tuesday of Lent
Babbling

Gospel: Matthew 6: 7-15

In your prayers do not babble as the pagans do.

Down from my Aunt Sarah's farmhouse in Ireland, along a path beside a meadow, you will come to the Glencullen River. If you make your way down there on a still summer morning, there is not a sound in the air. Then, at a particular spot halfway down the pathway, you will begin to hear a noise. It is the sound of the river, its shallow waters babbling over shiny stones in the riverbed. That noise and that babbling have been there all the time, but their sound reaches only to this spot. The trout river is in many places a deep brown colour, especially where deep pools of water gather, but down here, where it curves past my Aunt Sarah's meadow, the water is ankle shallow. It is clear and bright and it babbles all day long. As you come away from the river and back to the farmhouse, the sound of running water comes with you, until you reach that spot on the path, and suddenly it is gone, and the world is still once more.

It is that babbling brook that always comes to my mind whenever I hear the words of our Lord to his friends: 'In your prayers do not babble as the pagans do.' The world does a lot of babbling, and we do too. We use too many words and we use them rapidly, one word tumbling over another noisily, like water over shiny stones. We often think that the more we say and the faster we say it, the more other people will hear us and understand us. And we think the same about our prayers to the Lord. We might say reams of prayers, set formulas of address to God. In some cultures, just making a constant humming noise is regarded as a way of reaching the ear of the Almighty. But there is a better way.

The prayer that Jesus gives us – *Our Father* – is the perfect prayer. It is short and sweet and to the point. It sits perfectly in the stillness of our lives, just as the Glencullen River sits in the stillness of an Irish landscape. Out of the stillness of our hearts this prayer can rise each day. The words Jesus gives us to say carry the sound of our own lives up to the Lord and out into the world. All who live within hearing distance of our lives will be affected by every word we utter this day. If our words are kindly words, patient words, loving words, then the sounds we make in this world will give joy to all who hear us. Not all babbling is boring. The babbling of the river is a beautiful sound in the quiet of a summer's morning. But the incessant babbling of the human tongue can be a brutal and wearing sound to suffer.

The words we say need the silence of another's heart in order to be heard. The heart of God is forever still to listen to the words we offer him. What will we say to the Lord today, and why will we say it? Is there something you want? Say it. Is there something you are grateful for? Say it. Is it good simply to know the Lord? Then say it. But why? Why say anything at all? Because our words carry our very selves – our hearts, our intentions, our needs, our hopes, our desires – out from ourselves and into the lives of those who hear us.

To be able to express myself, and to express myself well, is to grow in stature as a human being. To learn how to speak to the Lord in a good way is to learn how to speak to all other people in the same good manner. My conversation is the extension of my prayer. It is the same sound that carries through the air. If I address the Lord with honour and worship, I will most surely address others with the same sense of honour and respect. Most of all, my prayer is an act of love for God, and such an act deepens my ability to love others. The words of the Lord's Prayer are all words of love, words of justice and words of truth. The grace that they seek from the Lord is the grace to live an honest and loving life, and to grow especially in the power of forgiving others their sins. If we persevere every day in the faithful utterance of this prayer, our words will become our deeds. Word and deed will become one and the same thing. My word will become my bond.

From my childhood in the 1950s, I remember many cowboy films where a meeting between white men and native American Indians always included the words of the Indian chief, 'White man speak with forked tongue.' The Indian in the film might not always have possessed perfect English grammar, but he knew the difference between truth and falsehood. Words are meant to carry us truthfully into each other's lives. For our Father in heaven, his name will be held holy if we speak the truth to one another at all times. His kingdom will come if we practise honesty and fairness all through our lives. His will shall be done if we consider others equally with ourselves in all our doings.

As for our own needs in life, daily bread, forgiveness of debts and avoidance of all evil is our common agenda. To pray for this each day is the sweetest babbling noise we will ever make. That noise will carry up to the Lord and he will hear it. Each morning the Lord comes out for a walk through the meadow of this world. At a certain point on the path he comes within hearing distance of our babbling life and he listens for the sweet music that we make.

Let our babbling be beautiful.

'The eyes of Yahweh are turned towards the virtuous, his ears to their cry.' (Psalm 34:15)

First Wednesday of Lent

A simple sign

Gospel: Luke 11:29-32

This is a wicked generation; it is asking for a sign.

I was born in 1947. The wicked generation had just come to a halt. All those wicked years of war, from 1939 to 1945 and before that from 1914 to 1918 – all those years were now at an end. Not that warfare ended; far from it – Japan, Korea, Suez Canal, Vietnam, Cambodia, Rwanda, Iraq, Iraq again, Afghanistan: these places and many more all over the globe have seen more than their share of suffering. In all the years since these terrible events took place, we, the children of the media age, the age of instant communication, have been able to watch and study many films and reports about the wars that have taken place.

From our vantage point of hindsight, and with all the help of research studies, we are able to see very clearly the faults and failings of those generations – the mistakes they made, the false mentalities they followed, the force of human influence to carry the day and to carry people away into bloodshed and human tragedy. After the carnage of World War I, the parties who met together and made a treaty of peace – the Treaty of Versailles – treated Germany very harshly, and thereby unwittingly sowed the seeds of further conflict and of the rise of Adolf Hitler. A basic thing like geography had a bearing on the thinking and feelings of the parties. France, being a border country to Germany, felt very strongly its need to protect itself by punishing its neighbour, whereas Great Britain, feeling more secure being surrounded by its seas, was inclined to wish for a more lenient treatment of its foe.

When our generation comes to be studied as 'history' by later generations, what will they say of us? What faults, what weaknesses, and what downright wickedness will they be able to find and point out? Sometimes we do not need to wait until a later date to examine and discover our faults. Indeed, it is the role and the task of any prophet, of any gifted person with insight, to try and speak to us of our wicked ways, and of our blindness, and to turn us towards the good.

Crowds of people come in their droves to listen to Jesus, the new preacher, and when the crowds increase greatly, Jesus turns to them and addresses to them some home truths. Chief among them is their reluctance to accept a person on the evidence of his life and his words. Such ordinary human evidence, which in normal circumstances we rely on to make judgements about people, is suddenly suspended in the case of Jesus. The people want miracles, entertainment, something out of the ordinary. But Jesus has not come to entertain people, although in fact he is very entertaining in all the good senses of that word. He has come to call people to a better way of life, to a life that is open to God. That is a demanding thing to do, and people are very slow to respond. They feel just fine as they are. Why should they change or try to be better than they are? Why should they commit to following this man and his teaching?

It is as if, like a modern crowd, they are chanting repeatedly, 'We want a sign! We want a sign!' The sign is right there in front of them – the man Jesus – yet they do not recognise him at all.

And what of us today? What is the wickedness that goes on that we do not see, or do not truly address? Perhaps it is the very same fault that Jesus saw in his own time and among his own people. We are people who are always looking for a sign. We are looking for something to entertain us, to distract us, or to convince us that we ought to do more than we do. We do not respond to the Lord who speaks to us each day. We watch. We wait. We listen. We do nothing.

And all the while, wicked things go on. Ours is the generation of abuse. We abuse and misuse everything – abuse of children, abuse of women and children, abuse of wealth and power, abuse of language, abuse of relationships, abuse of media and communication, abuse of all the good gifts that God gives to us when we simply use them for our own pleasure.

There is no end to the catalogue of crime and wrongdoing in the world. It was ever thus. But there can be an end to our own wickedness, to our own faults, to our own lazy refusal to budge. Is the word of God enough for me now to shift myself from my lazy ways and to live a daily life of response to God's love? Or am I still waiting for something to happen before I move myself?

Lent is a good time to make a renewed effort at life. Now is the acceptable time. This is the day of salvation. Oh that today you would listen to his voice. Today and every day is the day of the Lord. He stands before us and calls us; he speaks to us.

We, the followers of the Lord, do not ask for a sign. We already have a sign – Jesus and his cross. In the life of the Emperor Constantine a great story relates how he saw a sign in the heavens that promised him victory in battle. It was the sign of the cross. This is the sign already given to us and which we gladly and humbly follow. Each day we set out to follow the Lord and to walk in his ways, and to live in the sign of the cross, the Father, the Son and the Holy Spirit. Amen.

> 'God, create a clean heart in me, put into me a new and constant spirit.' (Psalm 51:10)

First Thursday of Lent

Good things

Gospel: Matthew 7:7-12

How much more will your Father in heaven give good things to those who ask him?

A BBC television programme, *Heir Hunters*, has introduced us to the concept of *bona vacantia.* This Latin phrase stands for 'ownerless goods' or 'unclaimed goods'. People who die without leaving a will often leave money and property behind which, if not claimed after due time, will go into the coffers of the government. The above-named heir hunters are firms who use their expertise and staff to research and find lost relatives who may be entitled to claim those unclaimed goods.

Bona vacantia, unclaimed goods, would be a good name for all the gifts of God that could come our way if we would only look for them, if we would put our energy, like heir hunters do, into the work of searching and seeking out, and knocking on doors. God has many good things to give to us, Jesus tells us today, but these good gifts go unclaimed because we do not ask for them.

In this famous teaching Jesus gives us a great three-liner by which to remember the importance of prayer of petition: 'Ask, and it will be given to you; search, and you will find; knock, and the door will be opened to you.' We never forget this sentence – it is so memorable. We only forget to carry out its instructions.

Jesus follows up his sharp sentence with a good story, like the good teacher he is. He talks about fathers and sons, parents and children. If your child wanted bread, would you hand that child a stone? If your child wanted some fish to eat, would you give that child a snake? If frail and weak and sometimes wicked people still know how to be kind and caring towards their children, what do you think your Father in heaven is like?

Then, as in all good stories, Jesus delivers the powerful punchline! If you can be good, how much more will God give good things to those who ask him!

This teaching of Jesus is simple, direct and makes powerful claims, and in the main many people ignore it. They do not believe prayer makes any difference whatsoever. They think prayer is never answered, and that spending time in prayer is a waste of time. So we must ask ourselves today, what are these good things that Jesus is referring to? What are those unclaimed goods, those *bona vacantia* that sit there waiting to be asked for?

We are talking now about spiritual gifts, things that enhance our ability to be good and happy human beings. These are gifts that Jesus often imparted through his preaching. The crowds that came to listen to him, in their thousands, knew they were on to a good thing: 'This man Jesus inspires my life.' The disciples spent three years in his company and they were enthralled by Jesus' words. 'Lord, who shall we go to? You have the message of eternal life' (John 6:68). Even the soldiers sent to arrest Jesus in the streets of Jerusalem came back to their superiors without a prisoner, and explained, 'There has never been anybody who has spoken like him' (John 7:46).

So in our prayer, through Jesus, the Father wants to share with us the gifts of the Holy Spirit. These are the 'good things' to which Jesus is referring when he instructs his disciples to pray. The list of good things is impressive, and seven gifts of the Spirit are identified as wisdom, understanding, counsel, fortitude, knowledge, piety and fear of the Lord (see Isaiah 11:2-3). Added to that list of gifts are the fruits of the Spirit that we can also ask for and receive. These are love, joy, peace, patience, kindness, goodness, trustfulness, gentleness and self-control (Galatians 5:22-23).

If your life possesses any of these gifts and virtues, you are a happy person. Now, our challenge and our need is to grow into all of these virtues and gifts, and they are there for the asking, the Lord tells us. As long as there is breath in our body we have a road to travel and good things to receive: good things not only for our own benefit but, equally importantly, for the blessing of this world. And our Father in heaven wishes to spread these good gifts among all his people.

We need wise leaders to guide nations and peoples into the ways of peace. We need understanding people to help those who are in mental suffering and stress. We need the gift of counsel to be able to advise one another on the road of life. We need people of courage to face and confront wickedness in the world. We need knowledge so as not to be walking in darkness. We need piety to inflame our hearts with love. We need the fear of the Lord to live our lives with due respect for God's truth.

As for the fruits of the Spirit listed above, look at them again now and you will see that any person who possesses even a 'smidgen' of these gifts will be a tremendously happy person.

In the work of *Heir Hunters*, a great deal of effort has to be made to try and identify possible heirs, and then to locate them. Hours of work are involved, and painstaking labour, before a travelling representative finally knocks on a door. A lot of asking, a lot of searching and a lot of door-knocking are done.

In the same way, the Lord urges us to the great work of persevering in prayer. Don't give up, he tells us. Seek the Lord every day and speak with him. You will never go away empty-handed. The gifts of the Lord he earnestly wishes to give us. They are so good, and they will change our life so much, it would be a shame to leave them lying there unclaimed. In our prayer life, let there be no *bona vacantia.*

> 'The day I called for help, you heard me and you increased my strength.' (Psalm 138:3)

First Friday of Lent

Love offensive

Gospel: Matthew 5:20-26

You have learnt how it was said to our ancestors: You must not kill.

The centenary of the First World War invites us all to look back at that catastrophic time and to try and read and interpret correctly the story we find there. History and hindsight can teach us many lessons if we are prepared to be ready listeners and learners. A word that jumps off the page of any history book of that sad time is the word 'offensive'. In military language, this is the taking of aggressive, forward action against the enemy, striking first and with speed to catch the opponent unprepared and certainly unable to repel the power and force of offensive attack. In the years leading up to the Great War, this mindset was commonly held by all the military nations of Europe, and so when trouble began, the headlong rush into open-armed conflict was guaranteed.

But the world had changed and military weapons had developed, and when such offensive attacks were made, soldiers found themselves heading into a hail of machine-gun fire, to be mown down as a machine threshes a hay field. Offensive action ground to a halt and, digging themselves into the muddy fields of Flanders, soldiers found themselves in trenches, and the warring nations found themselves 'entrenched' in hostile confrontation with mounting casualties and no victories to cheer them.

Offensive action was seen at its most effective at the beginning of the Second World War, when Hitler's *Blitzkrieg* attacks swept Germany on to swift victories. Meanwhile, remembering the lessons of the First World War, Britain and France concentrated on defensive action to begin with in what became known as the Phoney War.

In human relationships, the word 'offensive' is never anything other than a negative reality. To speak offensively or to act in an offensive manner is to hurt and wound another. An offensive person is a very unpleasant character indeed. Only in situations of war, which is itself an evil, can the word 'offensive' be regarded as a positive thing. To offend is to wound, and that is always wrong.

When Jesus looks at the old commandment, 'You must not kill', he will not settle for a limited understanding of this command. Instead, he takes us into the depths of human relationship and tells us that any form of offence against another person is unacceptable. To speak offensively, to ridicule, to slander, to hate, to be angry – none of these will do. And if we think we can approach God and be at peace with God when all the time we are at war with someone else, then we must think again.

Our social world and all our human relationships resemble a battlefield, and the amount of offensive behaviour that goes on is endless. The daily battle for the follower of the Lord is to bring hostilities to cease. Ours is the role of peacemaker. In the midst of conflict we are medical orderlies and our station is a field hospital. That is the Christian calling.

But this calling does not simply happen. There is training to be undergone if we are ever to know how to be agents of peace in a world of war. Jesus indicates this to us when he says to his disciples, 'If your virtue goes no deeper than that of the scribes and Pharisees, you will never get into the kingdom of heaven' (Matthew 5:20).

In conflict situations, then, what are the virtues we need if we are to become agents of peace? Perhaps the first thing to be said is that in our battles with one another, the purpose of our efforts is not to defeat our opponent but to win them over. We do not seek to beat our enemy but to find a peace between us. As we seek a change in our opponent, we will also be prepared to change ourselves.

When my son was younger and he and I had a difference of opinion, Michael would say to me, 'I'm right. You're wrong. Accept it!' It has become our catchphrase now. Humour then and humour now have helped us to negotiate our way with one another. There is no point in winning an argument if the price you pay is the loss of friendship.

When I was a child, my sister and I went for a walk through the fields with our collie dog, Bruce. Suddenly we found ourselves arguing over whose dog he was. I placed the dog in the middle of the road and my sister and I stood ten yards either side of him and began to call his name. The dog looked very sadly at each one of us, as only collie dogs can do, and then slowly and reluctantly came in my direction. My sister cried and walked home by herself. The dog did not look too pleased either, and I felt horrible. I never did that again. Love is meant to be shared, not divided.

When Jesus speaks to us of virtue, he is not referring to a pleasant attitude, but to a strength of soul. Virtue means power; it has nothing to do with being nice. Being nice will not see us through the battles of this life. Patience, understanding, confidence and perseverance are the qualities that are going to count.

In life it is good to have heroes, examples of goodness that we can look at and follow. There is no finer example for us than the Lord himself, whose every encounter in the Gospel story shows us a man who is able for others – friends, strangers, even enemies. He meets them all with goodness, fairness and courage.

And the Lord is not just our example. He is our living power. Living in his grace, and constantly seeking his grace, brings us into a life of joy. In Christ our Lord we learn to employ the greatest offensive action of all – the offensive of loving others.

'It is with Yahweh that mercy is to be found.'
(Psalm 130:7)

First Saturday of Lent

Enemy action

Gospel: Matthew 5:43-48

Love your enemies and pray for those who persecute you.

My father spent six years fighting in a war against the Germans. It wasn't personal. He did not know any German people at all. If he did have something personal against them it would be that of prolonging his service in the army, which had been due to finish in 1940 after six years of regular service. As he came near to the end of his initial contract, my father had a letter of recommendation in his pocket with an encouragement to report to Arsenal Football Club on his return to England from his posting in India. That never happened. Mr Hitler saw to that.

When the war was over, my father was based in a little town called Wolfenbuttel in northern Germany. They were helping to clear up the rubble of the war, and they were making a football pitch in the town for everyone to use. A young German lad was working there, and when it came to lunchtime, the boy sat down with the English soldiers to eat. Some soldiers began to curse him and tell him to go elsewhere, but my father intervened. 'He's a human being like us,' my father said, 'and he's worked all morning like us. Let him alone.'

When my father died and was buried, his son-in-law, Karl Heinrich, a son of Dusseldorf, placed a beautiful lantern on my father's grave, as is German custom. It looked lovely there, until some local came along and stole it. If it is true that a stranger is simply a friend we have not yet met, the same can be said of our enemies, whatever has caused hostility to arise and to cast us as enemies of one another. The truth is deeper, and the truth we must search for until we find that we are all human beings, sharing the same nature, and we are all children of the living God.

The soldiers of the First World War who found themselves in trenches at Christmas time in 1914 knew instinctively that war was crazy and that human nature belongs to us all. A German soldier, in the still of the night, began to sing 'Stille Nacht', and a British Tommy replied with 'Good King Wenceslas'. During that dreadful war, the sun rose and the rain fell equally on German and on Allied lines alike.

The history of the twentieth century is one of enemies and of how they brought death and destruction to millions of people. For us now, in the twenty-first century, there are precious lessons to be learned about how not to regard others as a foe and, where foes exist, lessons in how to negotiate with one another until the hostility is taken out of our relationships. It has never made sense to go to war as a good or positive choice; even less so now.

But we know that wars will continue to happen because we will continue to fail to learn how to resist them. New pressures in new world situations bring the old challenges to us in new clothes. Today, western democracies and Arab dictatorships look askance at one another. Different cultures struggle to understand one another. We should not be surprised. Every generation needs to listen afresh to the words of Jesus – 'Love your enemies and pray for those who persecute you' – and to learn how to put these words into practice.

Jesus reminds us how easy and normal it is to love those who love us. Anybody can do that. Al Capone did that. But to love those who do not love us – this calls for us to rise above the common routine and to cause a revolution. It calls us away from tribal habits of mind, from inherited traditions and from the poverty of a narrow vision. People who love their enemies are true revolutionaries, and they change the face of the earth.

Mohandas Gandhi in South Africa and in India brought social and political change to those countries by developing his understanding and practice of non-violent resistance to unjust laws and governments. Martin Luther King, greatly influenced by Gandhi, led the great movement for racial justice in America. Archbishop Desmond Tutu encouraged the practice of Jesus' words by quoting a comical saying: 'Love your enemy. It will ruin his reputation!' For militant people feed on militant resistance, finding in it a further reason to be unjust. Non-violence, on the other hand, like the art of jujitsu, uses the enemy's force against them to unbalance them and bring them down.

In that very vein, Jesus gives practical examples on how to love your enemy. If he slaps you on the right cheek, present him with the left. If he compels you to go a mile with him, go two miles willingly. Take the initiative in kindness. It will work wonders.

In the days of the early Church, the great apostle to the gentiles was Saint Paul. Here was a man of power and energy who, before his conversion, was ruthless in his pursuit of the followers of the Way of Jesus. All his energies were devoted to rooting them out and destroying them. When the light dawned on him on the road to Damascus, at first blinding him and then giving him new sight and insight, Paul became the greatest practitioner of loving enemies. I will, he said, make myself all things to all people that I may win some at any cost (see 1 Corinthians 9:22-23). Paul had discovered that the way of the crucified was the way to glory, and that human energy expended in narrow enmities and sectarian fighting was a blind alley leading into the darkness.

God is light and in him there is no darkness at all (see 1 John 1:5). The Lord calls us to live our lives in the light. It was dark in Gethsemane when his enemies surrounded him, and darkness fell over the whole land when Jesus died on the cross. But Easter morning came, and darkness is defeated.

> 'How happy those of blameless life who walk in the Law of Yahweh!' (Psalm 119:1)

SECOND WEEK OF LENT

Second Sunday of Lent

Who are you?

Gospel: Mark 9:2-10

This is my Son, the Beloved. Listen to him.

He would be sitting there at the fireside whenever I came home to visit. My father. I was the black-clad Catholic priest, filled to the brim with philosophy and theology, and he was the retired coalminer and ex-soldier. I was the guy who went to Rome and did further studies and came back with a degree in Moral Theology. I was now a professor and in charge of students, and there beside the fire at home sat my old man, frail now, and worn out by life. But whenever I looked into his eyes, or just quietly watched him as he studied the 'gee-gees' for the day, I knew I was looking at a wise man, a man who knew more about life than I ever would. His schooling had been the world itself, with its poverty and its hard work in dark places. His further education had been in the army, and his higher degree was received during six years of war. His professorship was lived out as a husband and father of four, after he came back from the war and went back down the pit. Now he sat by his fireside, drank his tea and gazed out of the window. But what a world lived inside that man!

We do not know the depths of any person, but oh what depths there are! We are mysteries to one another; indeed, we are often mysteries to ourselves. Who is this mysterious person 'I'? And this mysterious 'You'? We take some getting to know, unfolding and growing with each passing day. As children we love the adventure of living, but we also become aware of how little we know about life, about this world, about other people. It is part of life's attraction that there is so much to find out and to discover. And so we go to school and we begin.

When Jesus begins his public preaching life in Galilee, people gather round to listen to him, intrigued first of all by the attractiveness of the man and what he has to say. 'Who is this man?' they wonder. 'Where does he come from? How did he get all this knowledge?' Certainly, they are impressed by Jesus, but also they are bemused by him. They cannot fathom him. To begin with they are favourably impressed, and Jesus receives good reports. But public opinion is easily swayed and very changeable, and the days will come when Jesus' popularity will tumble.

Among his close friends the same sort of variability can be found. The disciples of Jesus, captivated by the young preacher and healer, are unsure exactly who Jesus is. They just know that they like him and they like to be with him, and they want to follow him. But when Jesus asks them directly, 'Who do you say I am?' they are not sure what to say.

But Peter does. Sometimes we do not know exactly what we think about something until the direct question is put to us, and then to our own surprise we hear ourselves coming out with an answer that we have never given voice to before. So it is on this occasion. Peter speaks up. 'You are the Christ,' he says, 'the Son of the living God' (Matthew 16:16).

This is a pretty amazing statement, and it must take Peter by surprise as he says it. And it is a pivotal moment in the story of Jesus and Peter, for Jesus confirms Peter in what he says, and thanks God for the revelation that has now been made. Jesus, for the first time in his public life, now feels himself to be understood. Peter has grasped something deep and true about Jesus, and Jesus is so grateful that this has happened. None of us in this world can feel comfortable if there is no one who understands us.

This insight given to Peter will now be strengthened and confirmed by Jesus when he takes Peter, James and John with him up a mountain. There, something quite out of the ordinary takes place. The man Jesus, whom Peter has declared to be the 'Son of God', now appears visibly in the glory that truly belongs to him as God's Son. And the disciples see this. It is a visible confirmation of the spiritual insight they have received.

Not only do they see something splendid, but they also hear something splendid – a voice saying from the cloud that covers them, 'This is my Son, the Beloved. Listen to him.' The disciples will hear many other things said about Jesus and against Jesus in the days to come – criticism, slander, rejection – but none of these will shake them away. They are followers of the Lord. They will also see terrible sights. Gethsemane and Calvary will shake them to the core. On the day when Pilate parades a tortured Jesus before the baying crowd and says, 'Behold the man!' there will not be any traces of a 'Son of God' to see.

The beauty they saw on the face of Christ on the mountain of the Transfiguration was annihilated by the brutality of his crucifixion on Calvary. Was this a Son of God or a poor, delusional creature? Certainly the Roman centurion standing by the cross had no doubt. He witnessed a poor creature being nailed to the wood, but the man he watched die became in his eyes truly a Son of God. He witnessed suffering transformed into something glorious.

In later days, Saint Peter will record for us what he saw in Jesus. I am not making up stories, he tells us. We saw his glory and we heard the voice speaking from heaven: 'This is my Son, the Beloved' (see 2 Peter 1:16-18).

There is nothing more glorious than persevering love.

> 'I will walk in Yahweh's presence in the land of the living.' (Psalm 116:9)

Second Monday of Lent

Fellow feeling

Gospel: Luke 6:36-38

Be compassionate as your Father is compassionate.

Many years ago, when I used to go to watch Bolton Wanderers playing football at the old Burnden Park Stadium, I would stand with my friends on the Burnden Terrace – these were the days before all-seater stadia. As soon as the match kicked off I would wait to hear a special shout. A man in the crowd would lift his voice as soon as a quiet lull came over the crowd, and he would roar out the famous words, 'Come on, Wanderers. Show them no mercy!' These were days when the Bolton defence was too generous in showing mercy to the opposition, and they needed reminding in no uncertain terms that a solid defence and no quarter given were the orders of the day.

I knew what mercy was, in theory. It was a form of kindness and consideration of other people and their feelings. I knew there was a religious order called the 'Sisters of Mercy'. I knew that Jesus was all merciful, kind and forgiving to all, and I knew that Roy Orbison said the word in one of his songs, when he sang 'Pretty Woman', after he had reached for an especially high note. But I also knew that I had come into this world just after the most merciless six years imaginable, when the world at war suffered terrible acts of unmerciful slaughter.

In particular, the unimaginable horror of the death camps, constructed and garrisoned by the Nazis, revealed to the whole world just how lacking in compassion and basic kindness human beings can be. Helpless, innocent people were sent in their thousands to the gas chambers – men, women and children. The masterminds of this cruelty kept their distance from the brutality that they ordered, and the staff of the camps could turn away their gaze, saying that they were only obeying orders. And some people just surrendered themselves to evil, even taking delight in what they did. Fellow feeling had died a long time previously.

And fellow feeling is the phrase. As human beings of the same flesh and blood as every other human being, we know what it must be like for another person because we know what it is like for ourselves. If we see another person happy and joyful, or sorrowing and sad, elated or depressed, we know what that is like, because we experience these same feelings ourselves.

When I was a child at school, standing in line, if a fellow pupil was being told off, I used to blush with embarrassment for them. As I think of that now, I think it is a wonderful gift of our nature to be able to experience tender feelings for another person. It is what makes for the bonds of humanity between us. To be compassionate is not a strange request that the Lord makes of us. It is to adhere to our truest nature.

When Jesus preaches his great sermon, which we call the Sermon on the Mount, he gives us four steps that follow on from one another. First, that we should feel for one another; second, that we should not think ill of one another; third, that we should not come to unfair conclusions about one another; and finally, that where wrongdoing has occurred, we should find it in ourselves to forgive one another. He then moves on to a fifth step, which switches from refraining from negative things to stepping forward positively to be generous in giving to one another. He tells us that the more we give, the more we will receive. This teaching of Jesus is not simply a list of good things to do; it is a 'step by step' programme.

In our troubled societies, there are many ills that call for our constant attention. Violent crimes, particularly, bring traumatic stress upon so many innocent people. In our justice system and in our medical society we try to address these issues and to understand the underlying causes that feed into violence. The words of Jesus here in his great sermon are powerful words to contemplate as we try to fit ourselves to face the ills of our day.

The Old Testament psalm (85:10) sings of justice and mercy meeting, and these two virtues stand together in our struggle to bring peace to our world. We live in a society that has abolished the death penalty, and this arrangement is a mercy, an unmerited gift. This decision in our society not only brings release to a guilty person; it also spreads in us a sentiment of kindness and tender mercy. Its effect is probably not even noticed among us. We just hear it as an element in our society's rules, but it is more than that. Even as people may rail against the cruelty and the nastiness of a particular crime and its perpetrator, still the fact that we choose to deal with this through the prison and hospital system helps a merciful character to develop in our public world.

In our television dramas we often receive good education about the hidden lives of people who go wrong, and these dramas help us to hold a more compassionate view of a particular wrongdoer. Surface information and tabloid headlines in our newspapers often do not carry very much in the way of truth in them. Compassion is often in short supply in the newspapers, and judgement there is a-plenty!

Condemnation is also to be found in our public discourse, and if capital punishment were to be brought back there are many who would advocate its use.

Short, sharp shocks and good doses of discipline are much favoured by many who would also regard compassion as silly, soft and nonsensical. But Jesus does not teach us one or the other. He teaches us to combine the power and the demands of justice with the kindness and the understanding of mercy.

Justice and mercy are not at war with one another.

> 'He never treats us, never punishes us, as our guilt and our sins deserve.' (Psalm 103:10)

Second Tuesday of Lent

Malachy

Gospel: Matthew 23:1-12

The greatest among you must be your servant.

There was a tattoo of an eagle on his hand, at the join between his thumb and his forefinger. I could see it clearly every time he came to our table to put a new loaf of bread on the bread board. As he grasped the loaf in his powerful hand and plonked it down in front of us, there was the eagle spread out before my eyes. I was a schoolboy in a junior seminary, and he was Brother Malachy.

He was a quiet, gentle man, humbly going about his daily work, which in this case was looking after the refectory – the dining room at the college – sweeping the floor after us messy boys, setting the tables for the next meal, and generally overseeing the operation of feeding hungry schoolboys. He was always pleasant, always had a ready smile, and he seemed to have oceans of patience and a great reserve of goodwill towards anybody who approached him.

But I also knew that this quiet man had quite an interesting history, although I only knew snippets of it. He was born in the west of Ireland and his given name was Patrick Kelly. He had joined the British army and had had postings in Austria, Jamaica and Germany. He had seen action in Hong Kong and then the big one – Korea. It was after his experience in the Korean War that Patrick decided to devote the rest of his life to God in religion. God knows what things he had seen in Korea, what things he experienced: old soldiers never say.

Three years after joining the Redemptorist Order as a lay brother, Patrick, now Brother Malachy, was putting loaves of bread down in front of my hungry, grateful face.

For the next 50 years, Brother Malachy lived a quiet and hidden life in the various houses of the Order, working as a farmer and a gardener and a sacristan looking after the church. His farms were energetically run, his gardens beautifully kept, his churches spick and span. And the man himself just grew in holiness of life. He never, ever said a bad word about anybody, though he was nobody's fool. His prayer life was non-stop, and as the years went by an inner brightness shone out of him that was evident to the human eye and to the camera. There is a photograph of Malachy in his later years, and the smile cannot be said to be *on* his face – it emanates from his soul, out through his eyes, and makes his face shine.

During his final illness, when he was in his eighties, a nurse in the hospital asked to be transferred to the ward where Malachy was for her weekend shift, just to be in his presence. She wanted the privilege of attending to a holy man. The quiet man who left his farm in Ireland and went away to fight in wars, who must have seen some terrible things, who came back and gave his life to God by serving other people, including little schoolboys hungry for bread, whom everyone called a 'walking saint', died in April 2011. He is buried in the monastery garden cemetery in Kinnoull, Perth, Scotland. I used to joke with him about that tattoo. Now the eagle has landed.

The life that Jesus calls us to is a life of service, to be servants of one another. This is one of the great paradoxes of life that the Lord taught: if you want to be first, then make yourself last. If you want to reign and rule, then make yourself a humble servant of others. If religion should teach us anything at all, it should teach us this, but as Jesus himself saw with his own eyes, religion tends to be used as a career ladder for self-promotion.

The Pharisees of Jesus' day seemed to set great store by how they looked and how others afforded them special privileges – wearing long tassels, and having the best seats in the house. If they had had mobile phone cameras, they would have been taking 'selfies'! Self-importance was their rule of life. Having a good public profile was their highest aim.

Being in positions of power and privilege, the Pharisees were influential in matters of law and order. They would be very concerned to see that law and order were obeyed and that the status quo was not threatened in any way. Self-preservation and self-promotion was all they cared for. With such a mentality they would have no notion of how hard it was for the rest of society to get by. Jesus pointed this out to them vigorously when he famously said, 'They tie up heavy burdens and lay them on men's shoulders, but will they lift a finger to move them? Not they!'

The Pharisee mentality is not confined to Pharisees. It lurks within us all, and Jesus would call us away from its contaminating influence. Not for us the idea of being above others, or in any way disassociated from the common man. Following Christ means that all people are to be honoured, respected and loved. This is the way of the Lord, and so we come back to the first step in following Jesus: make yourself the servant of others.

This path of service is not a high road to anonymity or annihilation. Quite the opposite. It is through serving one another that we will find the fullness of our human life and happiness. In the great political struggles of our age, capitalism has stressed the promotion of the individual to the great loss of society, while communism has stressed society to the total suppression of the individual person. We have seen the havoc that both systems have produced.

The way of the Lord is the way.

Listen carefully to what he says. To want to be great is a good thing. To want your life to really happen is a wonderful desire. In order to achieve this goal, make yourself a servant of others, and love will flourish. Ask Brother Malachy.

'To the upright man I will show how God can save.' (Psalm 50:23)

Second Wednesday of Lent

Drinking the cup

Gospel: Matthew 20:17-28

Can you drink the cup that I am going to drink?

On 24 March 1980 an assassin's bullet blistered through the silence of a celebrated Mass and killed the priest who was at the altar. The priest who died that day was Oscar Romero. He was the archbishop of El Salvador, a country torn apart by bitter political struggles, a country where the government's own forces were carrying out atrocities and killing its own people. Romero, a conservative man by nature who was not given to rowdy reaction or trouble making, found himself face to face with the evil of an institutional killing machine and the trampling of human rights. He had no choice. He had to speak out for the sake of ordinary people.

Using the means of radio, Romero spoke to his people every Sunday at Mass. It cost him his life. On 7 January 1979 he said, 'My position as a pastor obliges me to solidarity with everyone who suffers and to embody every effort for human dignity.' Two weeks later, on 21 January 1979, he said, 'The psychotic campaign against Christian communities – isn't that persecution? Isn't the trampling of the people's human rights also persecution? The Church considers this its ministry: to defend God's image in human beings.' Shortly before his death he called upon the soldiers of the state to obey the higher voice of God – 'You shall not kill' – and not the commands of the government. This was the final straw. The assassin's bullet sought him out.

This dramatic story imitates the story of Jesus himself, who also found himself under threat from political enemies who objected to his public utterances which they regarded as destabilising to their society. Jesus knew that if he continued to preach the word of God, and continued to be thoroughgoing in his purposes, he would be made to pay the highest price. He would lose his life.

And so, while he was on the way to Jerusalem, he took his disciples aside, away from the crowds, and spoke directly and confidentially to them, trying to explain and to forewarn his friends of the trouble that lay in store. But it is not easy to help others to see difficult things. We resist the telling, as Peter did when he said to the Lord, 'This must not happen to you' (Matthew 16:22).

It was at that moment that the mother of the disciples James and John, with the most abysmally bad timing, came up to ask for a favour for her sons. Jesus, all patience in the circumstances, explains that special favours are not his to give. What is for sure is that any follower of the Lord will be asked to drink the cup of suffering, simply because anyone who tries to live a good life in this world will have to contend with all the evil and hatred that sadly thrives here.

In our own part of the world, in our western societies, we do not experience the dramatic persecution that confronted Oscar Romero. No one is actively persecuting the Christian Church where we live. And yet the words of the Lord hold true for us, too. There is a cup of suffering and we must be willing to partake of it. The present Holy Father, Pope Francis, who is very strong on issues of social justice, has said, 'Trampling on a person's dignity is a serious sin.'[3] Here

3. Biography of Pope Francis, available at http://www.vatican.va/holy_father/francesco/biography/documents/papa-francesco-biografia-bergoglio_en.html (accessed 11 April 2014).

the Holy Father is attempting to open our eyes to the attacks on human dignity that go on all around us, and to which we have grown accustomed as part of the lifestyle of our liberal western democracies.

There is much suffering in our society, and it takes many forms – the break-up of family life, the suffering of single parents, the hurt and harm done to children. Our ability to maintain kindly human relationships has taken a battering through the pursuit of individualism, and from the stress of trying to make ends meet in our high-pressured society.

Attempts to escape from pain, stress and suffering lead many people into the harm of alcohol and drug abuse. These and many other issues call us to play a part in the suffering of our fellow human beings. This for us is the cup from which we are asked to drink. Every one of us has gifts to bring to the task of alleviating human suffering.

In the 1960s, when I was a student for the priesthood, I had the chance to spend a summer break working with the Simon Community in Liverpool, a project that exists to help homeless people. It was a rude awakening for me. I had never 'roughed it' before, and living in that hostel/home was a real eye-opener. The philosophy of the community is one of love, tolerance, acceptance and self-help. It does not seek to change people but to give them the space and time to consider things for themselves, in the meantime offering them human warmth and comfort and shelter.

There is great wisdom in the philosophy of the Simon Community. Many people have had damaging experiences which make it hard for them to build good relationships. They often have unrealistic expectations of themselves, of other people and of social structures. Staying in a hostel can be an anonymous experience, and often brings more trouble.

Staying in a community, on the other hand, can help such people adjust to a more realistic life plan. The founder of the Simon Community was Anton Wallich-Clifford who, when an officer with the probation service, met many people who were living homeless in London. So many charity organisations begin in simple ways, from one person seeing a need and responding to it.

What is the cup of suffering that comes to me? What part does the Lord ask me to play in drinking that cup? Is it something in my personal story? Is it something in the world around me to which I could bring my help and expertise?

'Into your hands I commit my spirit.' (Luke 23:46)

Second Thursday of Lent

Rich man – poor man

Gospel: Luke 16:19-31

> *There was a rich man who used to dress in purple and fine linen.*

In the early 1960s a young man went busking around the streets of Paris. He met many wandering, lonely people there on those streets, and heard many stories of heartache and sadness. He came back to London, sat down and wrote a song, but he did not try to publish it at first – it just seemed too sad and melancholy. But eventually he was persuaded to publish, and the song became his most famous track. In fact, his name is synonymous with the song. His name is Ralph McTell and the song is 'The Streets of London'.

The lyrics of this song tell us stories of various characters that McTell met – an old man in a market, an old woman on the street, an old man in an all-night café, an old man outside a seaman's mission. And the refrain of the song challenges us to compare our own situation in life with that of these struggling people. We may think that life is hard and our situation lonely, but a walk through any town will open our eyes to the struggles that others have, and will help us to see ourselves in a far healthier and hopeful way.

Whenever we walk down a street and see people begging, we are careful not to be waylaid by them. Sometimes we are willing to give them some money; sometimes we buy their *Big Issue* magazine. Sometimes we walk by, unsure how such people can really be helped. As Jesus told his disciple Judas,

'You have the poor with you always' (Mark 14:7) and we will always have opportunities to try and practise charity towards them.

The practice of charity is well developed among us in our world, and people have their favourite causes to which they regularly give alms. Supermarkets, too, have realised how good it is to promote giving, and there are often charity boxes at the exits to their stores to which we can contribute when buying our own food.

The story Jesus tells us about a rich man and a poor man – Dives and Lazarus – contains many lessons. For example, the rich man in this story is so rich that his very luxury inures him against realising just how poor and suffering the poor man at his gate really is. Anyone seeing a fellow human being suffering would be naturally moved to want to do something to help. But if we have given ourselves over to self-indulgence, we will have cushioned ourselves against the slightest capacity for human sensitivity and compassion. When you are not sitting in a draught, you see no reason to get up and shut the door!

Excessive wealth is often an obscenity. The stately homes of England tell many tales of riches accumulated on the backs of working-class people who slaved in mines and factories for a pittance, while the owners of industry grew fatter and fatter. With the establishment of society into the haves and the have-nots there comes a mentality of prerogative which seeks to keep each group safely in its place. As the famous hymn 'All Things Bright and Beautiful' has in its third verse:

The rich man in his castle,
the poor man at his gate,
God made them high and lowly,
and ordered their estate.[4]

The parable that Jesus tells, using the figures of a rich man and a poor man, reminds us of the inequalities of this world and then of the injustices of this world. There are so many things that are 'not right'. Over the past hundred years, we have seen the world convulsed over this issue. The story of Russia is the story of the rich man and the poor man. It led to the overthrow of the monarchy and to the reign of terror of the dictator Stalin. Now that Soviet communism has been shown to be vicious, it would be a great mistake to think that unbridled capitalism is wonderful. It is not.

Pope Francis, from the word go, has embarked upon preaching a gospel of love for the poor. He has switched the Church's energies away from doctrinal niceties and rigours to the call of the Lord to love our fellow men, women and children. It is time to promote more vigorously the Church's social teaching. In particular, Pope Francis has spoken about the 'trickle-down theory' of economics, whereby prosperity, allowed to grow, will pour over and down to benefit the poor.[5] Oh no, said the Holy Father. What happens is that when the glass is full, suddenly the glass is made bigger and nothing ever comes out to favour the poor. His comments were labelled 'pure Marxism' by an American commentator![6]

4. Cecil Frances Alexander, 'All things bright and beautiful', 1948 (public domain).
5. Apostolic Exhortation *Evangelii Gaudium* (The Joy of the Gospel) Pope Francis, 24 November 2013.
6. Rush Limbaugh, American Radio host, see CNN Belief Blog, 2 December 2013. Available at http://religion.blogs.cnn.com/2013/12/02/rush-limbaugh-vs-the-pope/ (accessed 11 April 2014).

Jesus knew only too well the danger of riches. Remember the story he told of the rich farmer who had a bumper crop (Luke 12:13-21)? What was his response to prosperity? I need to build a bigger barn!

Back to our parable of Dives and Lazarus – what is Jesus trying most of all to say? He is pointing out how some people lose their sense and their sensitivity to their fellow human beings. They seem to think that it is all right to ignore human suffering in others. 'That's life,' they seem to say. 'Nothing to do with me!' And once they have shut the door on other people and other people's needs, nothing will ever get through. No message, no teaching, no feeling, not even if somebody came back from the dead to warn them! It would all mean nothing to them.

People who turn in on themselves and on their own well-being lose their humanity. They lose fellow feeling. Compassion is not a word they understand. Such people become 'heartless', and that is the kiss of death to their own souls.

Jesus points to Moses and the prophets as our help and guides. Moses represents the Law, which is our good teacher. The prophets are inspirational people who are given to us in every generation.

Let us listen and learn.

> 'Happy the man who never follows the advice of the wicked.' (Psalm 1:1)

Second Friday of Lent

Crazy paving

Gospel: Matthew 21:33-43, 45-46

It was the stone rejected by the builders that became the keystone.

When I was a child of seven, I accompanied my father to work. It was my very first job and I felt so proud to be walking beside my dad as he pushed a wheelbarrow along the road of our newly built, post-war estate houses. My father had gone on this errand at the request of my mother. She wanted to develop the garden at the side of the house, and she thought some crazy paving would do the trick. Just up by the fields a short distance away lay some general rubble that was accumulating as the house builders constructed new properties for the local people.

Arriving at this place of general rubble, my father started to pick through the rough stones and slates that he found lying there. I tried to help. When he had collected all that he needed, he sat down in the afternoon sunshine and had a cigarette. I sat beside him feeling very important. I was now a worker like my father. I did not go down the mine like he did, digging coal, but I helped to find paving for the garden – my very first job! It was a Sunday afternoon, as I recall, and my father's day off – his day of rest – but Mum's word seemed to be powerful, and so we workers set to.

It is an abiding memory with me. It was work. It was part of the adult world. It was something that my father did, and I wanted to be part of all that. I felt pride in being a worker, pride in doing something that big people did, and pride most of all in imitating my father, whom I loved.

In the parable of the vinedressers Jesus tells a story about work and workers, but there is precious little in it to be proud of. This story should be told in cinemascope, it is such a huge drama. It is a Charlton Heston-like story: a landowner who plants a vineyard and goes away, leaving his tenants to till the vines and produce its fruit and to pay their dues; tenants who turn resentful of their landlord and decide to renege on the deal. They mistreat all the delegates sent to them, and finally they assault and kill the landlord's beloved son.

Jesus invites his hearers to finish the story. 'What will happen now?' he asks. The listeners know the answer very well. The rebellious tenants will be brought to a sad end and the vineyard will be leased to others. At this point the story hangs in the air. Why have you told this story? Who is this story for? Who is this story about? All these questions hang there. The answer is quite devastating, and Jesus' listeners know it.

This is a powerful confrontation between Jesus and his opponents – the scribes and the Pharisees. They are standing together in the Temple, that fine building, that monument to Israel's faith, that building that one day will be reduced to rubble. What Jesus has to say to these people is a 'hard saying' – something very difficult to say, and almost impossible to hear. So to convey his message, Jesus does not point a finger at anyone. He does not create an atmosphere of contradiction in which his hearers could legitimately 'take the huff'. He tells a story. Let the story convey the truth, and let the hearer apply the truth of the story. A case of 'if the cap fits . . .'

When the penny drops, when his hearers have absorbed the meaning of the story, then Jesus gives them the bottom line: 'It was the stone rejected by the builders that became the keystone.' Jesus, the one the religious authorities reject, is God's true Temple.

Sometimes reading the stories in the Gospels can feel like reading about 'goodies and baddies'. And the poor Pharisees are the baddies. Well, it is true in this instance that the intentions of the Pharisees had turned murderous in relation to Jesus, but in the general run of the story, the Pharisees are often a good reflection of ourselves. They can hold rigid and unchanging attitudes. They can give importance to the wrong things. They can become blind to the real values of God.

In this sense, the Church stands always under the searching judgement of the Lord, and the Lord may well have occasion to tell us parables that do not do us any favours. An occupational hazard of any religious person is to become presumptuous about the things of God. When that happens we stop producing the fruit that God expects in our lives. Instead, we become keepers of a castle that no one wants to live in.

We are workers in the vineyard of the Lord. It is a most honourable profession. Indeed, it is the highest profession and the best work that there is – to tend the vines and to produce the fruit. In my childhood world I knew that work was an honourable thing, an important thing that helped to make life good for people. And to work with my father was the noblest calling of all. The crazy paving we brought home was set in place and looked great for years afterwards.

That is a parable of our discipleship with the Lord and of our daily life in the Lord's vineyard. It is good for us to stop and to remind ourselves each day that with the return of morning, we begin another day in the service of the Lord. It is our privilege to be here and to do the things that we do. In our care for one another, in the daily routines of our lives, we tend to the garden in our own corner of the world, and even our crazy paving can be beautiful and will last for years to come.

'Remember the marvels he has done.' (Psalm 105:5)

Second Saturday of Lent

Salvation story

Gospel: Luke 15:1-3, 11-32

A man had two sons.

When separating parents seek the help of mediation, the first meetings are individual interviews in which each one tells their story. When the mediator comes to read the reports he is always reminded of the saying, 'There are two sides to every story.' When the mediator then places the two reports side by side, he sometimes wonders whether these documents are reporting on the same events, so different is the telling. Indeed, they are the same events, but they are being reported from different points of view. A simple example will suffice.

On the morning of a handover of children from Mum to Dad, Dad arrives and steps into the hallway. Mum objects to this and motions him out. They argue about it. When they come to report the event, Dad says, 'I just stepped into the hall and she pushed me out!' Mum's version of events says, 'He tried to get into my house and I told him to leave.'

Both versions of the event are accurate reports, and they accurately convey the feelings that each party experienced on that occasion. Instead of one version contradicting the other or relegating the other to the status of a lie, the fuller truth is that both versions can sit side by side as an accurate description of what went on that morning. The whole truth is far greater than our own particular experience of it.

These thoughts will help us a great deal when we come to look once more at the story of the Prodigal Son. This tale that Jesus tells is wonderfully accurate in every detail in describing human life, human reactions and human feelings. And each event in the story can bear many interpretations, as life always does.

A young boy, keen for adventure, asks for his inheritance from his father and leaves the farm. He takes the money and runs. He leaves his older brother to shoulder the burdens. He forgets his father. Take your pick of interpretations!

When times become bad the boy comes to his senses. I have been a fool. Better to be a servant at home than a forgotten slave here. And Dad is kind anyway. Mixed motives at work, no doubt.

When the boy returns home, his father cannot contain his relief and his joy at seeing his boy again. A great celebration is organised. And that is when the elder son hears all the noise. When he learns the cause of the jubilation, older brother is not best pleased. And quite rightly! How would you feel? 'I have slaved all these years for you. I never put a foot wrong. You never gave me a party! Now the blue-eyed boy comes back after all his gallivanting and this is what you do!'

The story is so true. The elder brother has a point. In fact, he has quite a list of points! He can point to all the hurt and wrong that the young one has done – to his father, to himself and to the managing of the farm. 'Are you going to forget these things?'

The father's reply is instructive. He does not forget these things. He knows the hurts that have been done. He suffered them! But the question is, what is the most important thing in life? Answer: salvation. 'My boy was lost and is found. My boy was dead and is restored to life. The rest can wait. He can learn from his mistakes. The rest can fly away on the breeze.'

The father's instruction to his faithful son continues. Faithful you are, but grateful you are not. You regard your life as drudgery, here in the happiness of your own home. You may not have wandered far away to other lands like the young one did, but your heart has wandered far away from me, even so. You, too, need to find your way home.

This final reflection is hugely important for religious people. Our faults are not as easily seen or recognised by ourselves as are the faults and erring ways of others. The scribes and the Pharisees prompt this story out of Jesus precisely because they complain about the rough company he keeps, eating and drinking with sinners. Faithful keepers of the Law, these religious people seem to be blind to the hypocritical manner of life that they live.

In later Christian writing, Saint Paul says that the life and death of each one of us has an effect on others. Everything we say and do can bear so many different interpretations. We affect one another all the time. Jesus has such an uncomfortable effect on the Pharisees that they start to calumniate him. His healing work is ascribed to the work of the devil. To do that is to sin against all that is holy.

This story about the two sons is not a story about a good son and a bad son. It is about an adventurous son and a stay-at-home son. It is about boys who have different temperaments. Both have their qualities and gifts and both have their weaknesses and faults. The faults of the younger son are dramatic, glaring and obvious. The faults of the older son are hidden and unrecognised. The father does not have a favourite; he loves both his sons equally.

It is the same in life. Jesus does not divide his love. He does not hate the Pharisees. They, like the elder son, are trapped in their own self-righteousness. This is what makes it hard to get through to them. They think they never do anything wrong. They cannot be saved because they think they are above salvation.

And salvation is the thing. Nothing is more important in the world than that we should be saved. It is that love that led Jesus to the cross. As the psalm of old has it: 'He, Yahweh, is merciful, tenderhearted, slow to anger, very loving, and universally kind; Yahweh's tenderness embraces all his creatures' (Psalm 145:8-9).

'Yahweh is tender and compassionate.' (Psalm 103:8)

THIRD WEEK OF LENT

Third Sunday of Lent
Sacred space

Gospel: John 2:13-25

Destroy this sanctuary, and in three days I will raise it up.

Dresden. The sound of this word is very near to the sound of another word – dreadful. Dresden stands for all that is beautiful and for all that is terrible in our world. This German city in the province of Saxony was hailed for its loveliness as 'the Florence of the north'. The famous Dresden pottery is made there. But in 1945 this city – so far untouched by Allied bombing raids, and quickly becoming overcrowded as German refugees fled in the face of the advancing Red Army –was chosen as a target for terror bombing. The act was intended to destroy the morale of the civilian population and help bring the war to a speedier end. In the event, it was a raid that caused the most intense firestorm on the ground and burned thousands of people to cinders.

The bombing crews who went on these missions over Germany were usually given specific targets at which to aim – railway lines, goods yards, factories – but on this raid no target was specified other than instructions to bomb the city. The bombs dropped were incendiary bombs whose effect in creating a storm of fire was frightening. On this occasion, the death of civilians was not 'collateral damage'. Civilians were the target. It was criminal, and it troubled many of the aircrew. People sacrifice their lives in wartime, and many a noble story can be told of people doing the best they can in situations beyond their control. But killing other people never healed the world.

The redeeming work has been going on ever since. Volunteers from Coventry, a city that was also target bombed in 1941, went out to help build a hospital that had been destroyed by British bombs. The President of Germany visited Coventry on the fiftieth anniversary of its bombing and spoke of his nation's guilt. When the beautiful Frauenkirche in Dresden was rebuilt, a gold cross was made – a gift from the people of Britain – to adorn the dome. The maker was a goldsmith in London whose father had been in bomber command during that terrible raid.

This memory of Dresden leapt into my mind when I read the Gospel story about Jesus and the traders in the Temple. Asked by the Temple authorities to explain why he has driven traders out of God's house, Jesus replies, in mysterious words, 'Destroy this sanctuary, and in three days I will raise it up.'

Jesus knows that these religious people are plotting his death. There in the Temple they find themselves unable to arrest him, since the people as a whole are very impressed with Jesus. But they will come by night, and they will take him by night, and they will question him and brutalise him by night. They are experts at dark deeds.

And the day comes when, in fact, they do destroy the sanctuary of his own life. They kill him, and killing has been going on in every generation before and since. Human carelessness takes people's lives away through reckless driving on our roads; driving is a great killer and a bringer of great sorrow. Human anger, uncontrolled and unhelped, leads many into acts of manslaughter and murder. A firestorm of sorrow over the land. We stand in need of acts of healing and redemption.

Some friends of mine lost their son in a rage attack. He came upon a fighting incident between a man and a woman and the man turned on him and killed him. Today I received an email in which my friends tell me of the help they have found for their broken hearts in The Compassionate Friends, an organisation that cares for those who have lost children.[7] The murdered man's own children – my friends' grandchildren – have been helped by a grief counselling group in their local hospice.

We shall not be destroyed. Jesus, by his own death, has destroyed all death forever. After three days we shall be raised up. After a time of mourning and sadness, we shall come back to life. We live our lives now in the light of the Lord's resurrection. It does not mean we escape the sorrows and pains of this world, but it does mean that the Lord's light will always scatter the darkness, and no matter how bleak things may become, death and sin are defeated.

One of the great graces that can come to a people is the grace to abolish the death penalty. No matter how much others may deal out death to us, we will not deal out death to them at all. We deal in hope, in the hope that has been given to us by the Lord. We have still so many lessons to learn from the experience of the wars of the past century. The 'victors' were those who could sustain the greatest death-dealing weaponry over time. What kind of victory is that?

7. http://www.tcf.org.uk/ (accessed 31 March 2014).

Military 'mindsets' will only ever look for military solutions. But even military men know that 'war-war' has at some point to give way to 'jaw-jaw', as Winston Churchill conceded.[8] My own father, who served in the Royal Artillery throughout the Second World War, shook his head in sorrow when he saw soldiers being sent to defend the Falkland Islands. 'War is a mug's game,' he said. 'Nobody wins. Everybody loses.' I do not think there is any contradicting that statement. We know that war is foolish and that it solves nothing. The question is, 'What are we able for?'

Saint Paul's answer is before us. We preach a crucified Christ – God's foolishness – God's weakness (1 Corinthians 1:23-5).

The human sanctuary is to be reverenced. Each and every human being is a person to be honoured and respected. This is the Christian gospel. This is the Christian way. I have seen many fine churches and chapels in my life, from my own Lancashire parish church to the grandeur of St Peter's in Rome. The reverence shown in these sacred buildings is instructive. Treat one another with the same honour and consideration. We are holy ground.

'You, Lord, have the message of eternal life.' (John 6:68)

---

8. Attributed to Winston Churchill at a luncheon in the White House, 26 June 1954, and reported in the *New York Times*, 27 June 1954.

Third Monday of Lent

Sitting at Jacob's Well

Gospel: John 4:5-42

> *Come and see a man who has told me everything I ever did.*

In 1986 the singer Cyndi Lauper, famous for her feisty rendition of *Girls Just Wanna Have Fun*, released a song entitled *True Colours.* This song was written by Billy Steinberg, and he wrote it for his mother. Steinberg's mother had a rather difficult life and her son had often noticed her sad eyes, revealing, while hiding, the darkness inside her soul. Steinberg said that he could not remember a time when he saw his mother laugh, and yet he knew that his mother was a truly lovely person. Her true colours were beautiful indeed.

This song could well provide a soundtrack for the Gospel encounter of Jesus and the woman at the well. From reading this story we learn that this Samaritan woman has also had a difficult life. Married five times and now with man number six, the woman may well have a poor opinion of men, and probably with good reason. She would not be popular with the other townswomen, who would normally go together on the daily trek for water. This woman is on her own. She is a person to be avoided. She lives her days in the shadow of cynical disappointment.

At the well she sees a man sitting there, who by all accounts would not and should not talk to her. Rabbis do not speak to women in public places, and Jews do not speak to Samaritans full stop. Yet Jesus speaks to her, asking for a drink of water. Water – the most natural element that we all need to share in this life. Jesus begins to knock down all the barriers that supposedly keep this woman and this man apart – gender, nationality, religion and history – including the hidden barriers of human sadness, shame and disappointment in life.

Sweeping away all the barriers between them, Jesus and the woman now arrive at a place of simple truthfulness, and a time for personal self-revelation. This woman has lived with the burden of her history and the weight of other people's disapproval for too long. Jesus relieves her of that burden, telling her that he knows all about her past and he is still happy to associate with her. For the first time in her life the woman can stand in this world as the person that she is and not be ashamed. Here, today, beside Jacob's Well, this woman can stand in her true colours. And they can shine through.

In this exchange, not only does Jesus reveal her true self to this woman and show it to be beautiful, but he also reveals himself and his identity to her. 'The Messiah . . . I am he' (verses 25, 26). Letting people know who you are can be a risky business. Giving people some insight into your inner self needs to be done with care. Do not throw pearls before swine. We need to be able to trust people if we are to share something of our inner self with them. This is the gift that Jesus makes to this despised woman. Now her true colours will really shine through!

A meeting at Jacob's Well is a blessing that we all need in life. A place, a moment, a person, a meeting that allows us to be who we are and to say who we are and not be ashamed. In my own life such a moment came when, at a time of crisis, I was fortunate enough to be directed to counselling. Over the course of 15 months I was able to unravel my story and, with the help of a highly trained person, Clare, to realise my own authority over my life for the very first time. I was 45 years of age. I needed to talk to someone, and that someone was there to listen. Out of that experience I came to understand that none of us is able to live fully in this world until we know who we are and can say it out loud.

For Jesus himself this meeting is also of great value. Not only is he able to set this woman free from all that burdens her, but in return he receives the benefit of being able to share something of his inner self with another human being – the listening heart of a woman. All human encounters are two-way transactions, and blessings flow to both parties.

Like the disciples returning from the town, we have so many things to learn. Chief among them are the words of Jesus that true worshippers worship in spirit and in truth. We might translate this as 'from the heart and honestly'. True worshippers have God's Spirit in them, and that Spirit does not recognise barriers of gender, nationality or religious tradition. If any of these elements separates us from others, then there is something not right about ourselves. Jew or Samaritan, Catholic or Protestant, believer or non-believer – these are not barriers to God's love. They are only human differences.

The woman at the well knows her religion very well. When the Messiah comes, he will tell us everything, she says. Yes, the Lord makes all things plain, and all things will be restored in Christ. As we read this story we are sitting beside Jacob's Well ourselves, and we are drinking from this everlasting spring that is Christ Jesus himself. And the Lord can tell us everything that we have ever done in our life, for the Lord knows us through and through.

And we are not condemned. The knowledge that Jesus has about us all is saving knowledge. This was enough to bring the local townspeople out to see this man at the well. Invited to stay, Jesus remained there for two days – long enough for the people to get to know him and to believe in him.

'Let us . . . kneel in front of Yahweh our maker.'
(Psalm 95:6)

Third Tuesday of Lent
I beg your pardon

Gospel: Matthew 18:21-35

> *Lord, how often must I forgive my brother if he wrongs me?*

'Our relationship broke down,' the man said, as he explained his situation to the mediator. 'That was bad enough. But then she took my son away from me and I will never forgive her for that.' It was a sentiment that the mediator did not wish to hear. When you refuse to forgive another person for some hurt done, when you say that you will never forgive them, you lock yourself into a prison of unhappiness and frustration just as surely as you intend to enclose another in that same darkness. Unforgiveness is not a power that you hold over another person, but rather a darkness into which both parties are plunged by such a choice.

As Jesus made his way from Galilee to Jerusalem, preaching and teaching, Peter is there at his side, listening and learning as best he can. He is a natural leader, somewhat impetuous by nature, and very strong-minded. Jesus makes some dark references to suffering which leave Peter confused, and on one occasion reprimanded. There is a lot of teaching about being like a child, and being a servant, and about compassion for those who go astray. But there remains a huge issue as yet unaddressed. What does Jesus have to say about dealing with this world's incessant wrongdoing? What do we do with persistent offenders – in personal life, and in public life?

Jesus has already had a discussion with the disciples about this very subject, and his teaching is very healthy. Speak openly to those who offend. Sort it out between the two of you. If the problem persists, ask the help of another person; take it to a wider group and to the community if necessary. The teaching is open and clear, but something is annoying Peter. Surely there comes a point when forgiveness must stop! Surely there comes a time when you just have to sort somebody out! It's a John Wayne moment.

This reminds me of a story my father told me. He was back from the war, a young father and playing football for a local colliery team. During the game an opponent kept tackling my father late, kicking him persistently throughout the game. The referee did nothing about it. So halfway through the second half when this guy did the same again, my father turned round and 'lamped him one', as they say. He laid him out flat. Then, acknowledging the referee, he began to walk off the field of play. 'It's all right, Ref,' said my dad, 'I'm going off. You did nothing about it, so I decided I would.' My father knew it was not the right thing to do, but his patience had been pushed too far.

Turning to answer Peter's question, 'How many times must I forgive someone?' Jesus says that this is not a numbers game. In the kingdom of God, forgiveness is part of the way of life. In fact, life cannot survive without it. Evil is such a terrible thing and the harm done is so hurtful and upsetting that only the grace and the healing balm of forgiveness can address and tend the wound that wickedness inflicts.

As I write these words, a great witness to the healing power of forgiveness has just died. Eric Lomax was a Scottish soldier during the Second World War. Captured by the Japanese, he worked on the infamous Burma Railway. His captors – in particular, one Japanese soldier – tortured him most cruelly. Lomax was deeply scarred psychologically and emotionally for years afterwards. He would willingly have killed that Japanese man if he ever found him. His mental agony gave him many problems. Eventually his wife arranged for a meeting, which took place in 1993. As the men approached one another, the Japanese man, Nagase Takashi, bowed low and with tears said, 'I am so sorry, so very sorry.'

Eric Lomax said, 'I had come with no sympathy for this man, and yet Nagase, through his complete humility, turned this around.' Both men, Eric discovered, had suffered deep psychological problems as a result of the war's brutality. Eric's wife asked him, 'What about the hate?'

Eric replied, 'Hating has to stop sometime.'[9]

The apostle Peter still has a lot of learning to do. In Gethsemane he is ready to fight and he draws the sword, but Jesus tells him to put it away. When Jesus' sufferings are over, in the day of his resurrection, light floods into the mind and heart of Peter, and he really does learn the way of forgiveness and pardon of crime.

If you take up and read the letters that Peter writes at the end of his life, you will see the teaching of the Lord fully absorbed and fully explained. Peter is the great preacher of Christ's peacefulness.

> No one can hurt you if you are determined to do only what is right; if you do have to suffer for being good, you

9. Robert Hardman, '"Some time the hating has to stop": A tortured war hero, his Japanese tormentor, and the redeeming power of forgiveness', *Mail* Online 10 October 2012. Available at http://www.dailymail.co.uk/news/article-2215357/Eric-Lomax-A-tortured-war-hero-Japanese-tormentor-redeeming-power-forgiveness.html (accessed 18 April 2014).

> will count it a blessing . . . If you can have some share in the sufferings of Christ, be glad . . . it is a blessing when they insult you for bearing the name of Christ.
>
> *1 Peter 3:13-14; 4:13-14*

This fine, brave man, at the end of his life, suffers the same fate as his Lord. He follows in the way of Jesus to the very end. As he says in his own letters, 'Christ suffered for you and left an example for you to follow the way he took' (1 Peter 2:21).

So Peter receives the answer to his question through watching his Lord suffer, die and rise from the dead. Evil and wrongdoing will not have the last word. God's grace is the last word. It is a grace that takes some learning, some acquiring. The pain of what we suffer is not made easier, nor is it healed, by adding more hatred or anger. And that is something that we have to learn. It is not so much a theory; it is a lesson of life. And it is a journey.

Jesus, the Lord of life, spoke the words that now guide our way. 'Father, forgive them; they do not know what they are doing' (Luke 23:34).

> 'Yahweh, make your ways known to me, teach me your paths.' (Psalm 25:4)

Third Wednesday of Lent
Law abiding

Gospel: Matthew 5:17-19

Do not imagine that I have come to abolish the Law or the Prophets.

In our schoolyard during the 1950s you could sometimes hear a conversation about religion. Being at a Catholic school, we children were taught our religion from *The Penny Catechism*, which was a question-and-answer-style booklet about the Faith. One of the things we were taught about in those days was a wicked thing called 'mortal sin'. If you died with mortal sin on your soul, you would go straight to hell . . . Do not pass go; do not collect £200. In the schoolyard a child could be heard to say, 'If that double-decker bus knocked you down now, with a mortal sin on your soul, you wouldn't be going to Bolton. You'd be going straight to hell!'

We also learned that one of the big mortal sins was missing Mass on a Sunday. So if you belonged to a family that was not gospel greedy and did not regularly attend church, the best way to avoid hell was to make sure you went to confession fairly soon, before you came into any kind of close proximity with a bus!

Rules and regulations were as thick as trees in a forest in those days. And because there were so many of them, it was hard to differentiate the important ones from the minor ones, and consequently, the mortal sins from the venial sins. In many ways, Catholic life in those days had become as cluttered with regulation as Jewish life in the days of Jesus.

The Lord himself was often checked by the Pharisees – for picking corn on the Sabbath, for healing on the Sabbath, or for not washing his hands properly. Jesus became so frustrated with his critics he had to tell them off for their pernickety observance of little rules while all the time they omitted the keeping of important laws. You are very good at keeping your dietary rules, he told them, but you don't mind defrauding old ladies of their wealth! (see Mark 12:40).

In the story of Israel, the Law is God's word, given for our instruction and guidance in life. Keeping God's Law will bring us happiness in the land where we live. Other peoples will come to see how beautiful this law is, and so Israel will become a light to the nations, an inspiration and an example. The Ten Commandments formed a great tablet of Law, expressing the most important things in life. They have not changed in all the years since. Lots of additions have been made as time has gone by, but these are time-conditioned rules, which can and should be changed as the years go by.

When Jesus comes and begins to preach, he says at the very outset that he has not come to abolish God's Law but to complete it, to deepen its meaning and understanding. And so in his great Sermon on the Mount we hear the refrain, 'You have learnt how it was said to our ancestors . . . but I say this to you' (Matthew 5:21-22). When the Law says 'You shall not kill', its truly positive intent is that we should love one another and not offend in any way.

A day comes when a lawyer, a well-trained expert in all the rules and regulations of the Jews, asks Jesus which is the greatest commandment (Mark 12:28-34). The answer Jesus gives is instructive: there is not simply one which is the greatest. There are two, and they are so intertwined that they then make one: to love God with all our heart and to love our neighbour as ourself. Nothing is more important in life than these two commands. How we fulfil them will lead us into recognising further commandments, and they will simply be further expressions of these two.

In human society, law is and has become our great protector. We live together as free citizens under the rule of law. This law not only calls us to account in our own lives; it also protects us from the abuse of power that so often threatens our safety in this world. When law and order breaks down, we are at the mercy of violent men and women. In earlier ages the whim and mood of the monarch could bring ruin and death to citizens. The struggle to make everyone equal under the law has been a long journey.

When Moses gave the Law to the Jewish people, he gave them a warning. Do not forget this Law, he said. Make sure you teach it to your children and to your children's children. Having a care for the law and making good laws is tantamount to having a care for one another. That is why Parliament is so important for the good care we take of one another in our society today.

In the UK we are very fond of crime and murder mysteries and of courtroom dramas. Among these, the series called *Kavanagh QC*,[10] starring John Thaw as a barrister, was a favourite. Thaw had already played the television detective, *Morse*, and so the image of a just man was firmly embedded in the British psyche when he came to play the barrister, Kavanagh.

It was the integrity of the character that Thaw played, as well as the public's love of the actor, that made for a very well-loved series. Practising law with integrity keeps it in

10. Central Television, 1995–2001.

good repute, and the words of Jesus could then well apply: 'The man who keeps [the commandments] and teaches them will be considered great in the kingdom of heaven.'

We live our lives under God's Law. It is not a burden. It is not imprisoning in any way. God's word spells freedom for us and leads us into the light. It has been a tragedy in the history of religions that often the Law has been used to tie people down. This has been a betrayal of the Lord, who has come that we 'may have life and have it to the full' (John 10:10).

'He reveals his word to Jacob.' (Psalm 147:19)

Third Thursday of Lent

A house divided

Gospel: Luke 11:14-23

> *He who is not with me is against me; and he who does not gather with me scatters.*

Fifty years have passed since the Great Train Robbery of 1963. That infamous crime, the halting and the robbing of the Royal Mail train of more than two million pounds in used banknotes, was masterminded by a man called Bruce Reynolds. His story is instructive about what can happen to anyone, for the story of our emotional development is the real key to understanding why we are the way we are.

Reynolds was only four years old when his mother died. When his father remarried, his new stepmother showed no affection whatsoever for the child. His childhood years were now emotionally torn apart. He spent much of his time in the care of his grandparents. When poor eyesight prevented his achieving his dream of joining the Royal Navy, Reynolds slipped into menial jobs and connection with petty criminals. The buzz of excitement from the experience of 'doing jobs' compensated for the lack of emotional stability in his life.

In prison, after the train robbery, Reynolds wrote constantly to his son to maintain that precious relationship, and it was a great joy to him in those later years that his son made a career as a diver in the Royal Navy. Reynolds' marriage had collapsed, but later he was reconciled with his wife. He regretted the hurt that had been done to the train driver, but he never regretted the course his life had taken. 'It was all part of making out that I was someone. But what I really liked about being a thief was that every week you might find El Dorado.'[11]

As we read this story now, it is easy to see the factors at work in this man's soul. The loss of his mother's love as a child, and this loss not being compensated for, left Reynolds vulnerable to other influences. The need that is in all of us to feel that we are someone, that we have human importance and value, was diverted in Reynolds' case onto the wrong track, if you will pardon the pun. Lots of money could not make up for a life derailed. His childhood home became a house divided, and young Reynolds never recovered from that.

Broken homes, divided families, separation and divorce are very common realities now in our world, and the sadness and suffering that proceed from them can be very upsetting for many people. But we need to be clear that the damage that is done to parents and children is caused not by people splitting up so much as by the continuing anger and hostility that they may direct at one another. Far better for a child that its parents separate and stop fighting than that they stay together 'for the child's sake' and expose the child to a continuing civil war in that house. How different Reynolds' life might have been if his stepmother had shown him love and affection.

The childhood of Jesus is described in the Gospel pages in one simple sentence. We are told that after he is reunited with his parents, having been separated from them for three days and then found in the Temple, Jesus goes back to Nazareth with Mary and Joseph and lives in obedience to

11. Bruce Reynolds' obituary, *Guardian*, 28 February 2013.

them, and as an old translation has it, he 'advanced in wisdom, and age, and grace' (Luke 2:41-52, Douay-Rheims Bible). This formula, so simple and so succinct, describes the best possible childhood experience we can have: as the years go by, in a safe and happy home, surrounded by love, to grow up in our understanding of the world and human society, and to grow in the virtues and temperament that enable us to stand with quiet calm and confidence among our peers in this world. If this has been our experience, we are the most blessed of people.

Many people, of course, it is sad to say, have very traumatic childhoods, and suffer greatly from neglect and abuse. Many of the problematic behaviours we see stem directly from such hurtful early experiences. This is why salvation is not simply a matter of education or teaching but, more importantly, it is a matter of healing grace. Jesus came among us as a preacher, a teacher and a healer. All three are vital to the work of salvation.

It was an act of healing that Jesus was doing when some observers accused him of doing the devil's work. He was enabling a dumb person to speak, and he was accused of being in league with the devil. Better for his accusers to be dumb than to use the gift of speech for such an evil and wicked accusation!

The harm done in this world every day by the things we choose to say is enormous. We live in a media world where talking is the predominant occupation. Talking, not listening. Carrying tales, not carrying kindness or understanding. The things we say to one another can cause so many houses to become divided. It would be good for us to learn to have some of that silence that belongs to those who cannot speak.

The work of healing is God's work, not the devil's, and we, as followers of the Lord, can play our part in healing the hurts of this world. The chief way in which we influence the lives of others is precisely in the things we say and the way we say them. We have great power over one another simply by the fact that we can speak. Our speech can bring joy to others or great sorrow, and this every day.

Just as we approach the Lord as a preacher and so learn the wisdom of the gospel, and just as we approach the Lord as a teacher and grow in our knowledge of life, so, too, can we approach the Lord as the healer, and ask his grace each day that our speaking may be a healing grace in the lives of everyone we meet. There is no sitting on the fence. Each day we do either God's work or the devil's. You can be a healer!

'If only you would listen to him today.' (Psalm 95:7)

Third Friday of Lent

The order of the day

Gospel: Mark 12:28-34

With all your heart, with all your soul, with all your mind and with all your strength.

After his beloved wife died, an old man looked around at his children and asked, 'What am I going to do now? I have all this love inside me and I do not know what to do with it.' Such is the wonder of our human nature. There is so much treasure inside us wanting to come out and to be shared. It is the way we are made, the way we have been created. If we are to believe the Scriptures, we have been made in the very image of God by God himself. That makes human beings something rather special. And what is this life of ours for? What is its purpose and its fulfilment?

In the Gospel story, Jesus is approached by a learned man, a scribe, who asks that very question. What is the first commandment of the Law? What is human life for? Jesus' answer is pure gold. To love, that is the purpose and the meaning of life. And to love with all your heart, all your soul, all your mind and all your strength. That is a lot of loving! And yet the answer is incomplete. The complete answer goes on to say, 'and to love your neighbour as you love yourself.'

The evidence of this world and of this world's history would tell us, in no uncertain terms, that we have failed to live up to these commandments in an abject manner. Something is seriously wrong with us, if we are created for such love, since everywhere you look there is so much pain, hurt and violence. It is no wonder, then, that many people are not impressed when they hear our religious language extolling the call to love. I remember a time when a friend of mine in religious life commented on the inconsiderateness of some members of the community. 'Christian brotherly love?' he scoffed. 'I'd be grateful sometimes for a bit of pagan civility!'

We find life to be very fraught – in our personal life, in our civic life and in the wide world of international relationships. Injustice, arguments, disputes and actual fighting are the order of the day. How can the love of God come into any of this? They say charity begins at home, and that is a very good place to start. Whether we are believers or non-believers – it makes no difference – our first duty in life, and we sense it in ourselves, is the duty to live an honest life: to conform our own life to all that is good, honest, just and true, in our personal conduct and in our human relationships.

In theory, this is wonderful. In practice, we find the world too troublesome, and before long we become as much a part of the problem as anybody else. The call of Jesus to follow him and to practise this love of God is most inspirational, but the world drags us down, and our own weaknesses add to its woes. In my own life I spent many years studying moral issues and preaching the gospel, but it took meeting the girl who would become my wife for me to really understand how to practise love in this world.

When my wife Margaret died, I realised that I had enjoyed a ringside seat beside someone who had known how to love other people, and how not to be brought down by them. I tried to capture this understanding in a few words at Margaret's funeral. The key word in Margaret's life was 'acceptance'. She accepted people when she met them. She always received them kindly. She was supportive in word and deed to people in her life. She was very honest with people. Sometimes being honest can cause problems, but people listened to Margaret because they knew they were already accepted for who they were. Finally, Margaret was able to challenge people when she needed to, without the challenge being destructive. With these qualities, Margaret showed me how to practise the love of God in this world.

This pen portrait is in fact the very same portrait that Jesus paints in the Gospel story, and the very same human dynamics are at work. We need to know and feel that we are accepted for who we are. We need kindly help and support. We need honest relationships, and we all need to be challenged at some time about something.

Sometimes in life the missing ingredient in our way of living is good motivation. We need something to burn inside us, something to set our hearts on fire. Why should I bother to go out of my way to help some people who do not seem to be worth bothering about? Very often our ability to care fades into nothingness the further it travels from our own lives. Why should we get involved in the business of a faraway country and a people of whom we know nothing?

For a religious person and a follower of the Lord, all the inspiration is there. We are children of the living God, and that makes us sisters and brothers one to another. The arms of Jesus, spread out on the cross, embrace the whole world and everyone in it. 'In so far as you did this to one of the least of these brothers of mine, you did it to me' (Matthew 25:40). The commandment to love is not so much a duty; it is the very meaning of our life.

Jesus' parable of the Last Judgement (Matthew 25:31-46) gives us the same answer to the lawyer's question in story form. The simple things we do – giving food to the hungry, drink to the thirsty, welcome to the stranger, shelter to the homeless, care to the sick and those in trouble – these simple things are the great achievements in any life.

'Let the wise man understand these words.' (Psalm 107:43)

Third Saturday of Lent

Mercy!

Gospel: Luke 18:9-14

This man, I tell you, went home again at rights with God.

In the autumn of 1964, at the tender age of 17, I travelled north from my home in Lancashire to join the Redemptorist Order and to begin my year of novitiate. This was a spiritual training year, to be lived in a monastery on a hill overlooking the 'fair city' of Perth. There was no academic study involved in that year, but rather a good deal of prayer and instructions in the Redemptorist way of life. It was a rarefied atmosphere in which to immerse young men, especially young men who had no experience of what it was to live in the world.

One of the spiritual teachings put before us in the many lectures we listened to was the idea of 'perfection'. In all the things we do and say we should strive to be perfect 'as your heavenly Father is perfect' (Matthew 5:48). The trouble is that 'perfection' is a dangerous word. It can set a person off on the wrong track. It can set a person on the road of individual self-preening, trying to make of oneself a perfect specimen of humanity. It tends to forget the social dimension of our lives as it trains the spotlight on self and on the spiritual progress that the self might make.

I remember now, with a smile, how one day I said to another novice who had recently arrived at the monastery how I had been trying all year to live a perfect day and that I had nearly managed it yesterday! To do all things well, and not have negative feelings or words with another – that was my programme. It was like walking a spiritual tightrope – very pious, very self-centred and not very helpful to a wider world.

This memory comes back to me now as I read the story of the 'Pharisee and the publican' who went up to the Temple to pray. The Pharisee in Jesus' story is full of himself and of all his perfect qualities. He really is a good guy and he knows it. He does everything right and he approves of himself with delight.

As he says his prayer of self-congratulation, he notices the tax collector at the back of the Temple, and he cannot help but make comparisons. Thank God I am not like that! This is a common enough feeling in all of us. When we see how some people conduct themselves, it is very easy for us to disapprove of their behaviour, and in the same breath to disapprove of them as people. To regard ourselves as being better than they are is an unconscious attitude and judgement that often develops within us. This is hugely dangerous and can have very negative repercussions in human society.

What is the truth about human beings, about all of us? We are not as wonderfully perfect as the Pharisee likes to think himself! But are we the opposite? Simply rubbish? Certainly not. As an old phrase has it: 'God does not make rubbish.' The truth lies somewhere in between. We are all of God's creating hand, and we are not yet the finished article. We are all good and we are all prone to selfish and sinful ways, and the story of our human journey, the things that happen to us, will greatly affect and even determine in many ways the kind of person we grow into.

Developments in medicine, psychology and sociology have greatly increased our ability to understand ourselves and our conditioning in life, and to see what factors influence our thinking and our acting. Our lives are interdependent. We are not separated, discrete units in an anonymous universe. We are of God's creating hand and we belong to one another. To think of oneself as being better than somebody else is a foolish, divisive and dangerous notion. Such an attitude has a name – despising – and to despise another is a form of condemnation. It is also a factor that leads people into open hostility and violence.

Back in the Temple, Jesus has great praise for the tax collector, not because of his lifestyle – which, presumably, leaves a lot to be desired – but because of his complete honesty with God in his prayer. He tells the truth about himself, and so, Jesus says, he is 'at rights' with God. A word that crops us here is 'humility'. An old priest used to say, 'Humility is like the soap in the bath. The minute you think you've got it, it slips out of your hand!'

Humility comes from the Latin word *humus*, meaning 'the ground'. As a virtue it is not a recommendation to crawl or grovel on the ground. Rather it is an invitation to stand with your feet planted on the ground, the ground of the truth about life. The truth is that life itself has come to us as a gift from the Lord, to be received with gratitude and to be lived honourably in love for God and for one another.

The person who truly knows that their life is a gift from God and accepts it as such will grow in grace and be exalted in virtue. Life will really happen then, and wonderful things will come. Humility is not a put-down or a depressant. Nor is it a killjoy. Quite the opposite: humility draws people in.

In the world of rock and roll, the figure of Roy Orbison stands out as a good and humble man. In a macho world, Orbison was different. He was quite prepared to sing about male emotion at a time when people did not do that. In his own distinctive voice he would sing of crying and feeling down. He opened up his soul and so gave people permission to admit their gentle and emotional side.

People still remember and sing the songs of Roy Orbison, but most of all they remember the man and his easy way and humble style.

'Have mercy on me, O God, in your goodness.'
(Psalm 51:1)

FOURTH WEEK OF LENT

Fourth Sunday of Lent

A sign in the sky

Gospel: John 3:13b-21

The Son of Man must be lifted up.

When I was a child, growing up in 1950s Lancashire, the first game I learned to play was Cowboys and Indians. That is perhaps strange in itself, since there were neither cowboys nor Indians of the Native American variety in my part of south Lancashire. But the influence of America was already strong in Britain, and the circulation of comics and of American films at the local cinema meant that we were well educated about such characters as Tom Mix and Roy Rogers and other heroes of the Wild West.

In the stories we read and the films we saw, the cowboys were usually the heroes and the Indians were reduced to the role of villains, swooping down on innocent wagon trains and meting out butchery on poor white travellers. My friends and I used to play in our back gardens, pretending to ride horses, rearing up and slapping on backsides as though on horseback.

The age-old struggle between good and evil was being played out in those childhood games, and everyone always wanted to be on the winning side and to be in the right. A boy in our road called John, a quiet-natured lad, was always given the role of an Indian or an outlaw, and always ended up dead. He undertook the part with obedient glumness.

As we grew up, we began to learn about more recent struggles of good and evil, since we were children of the immediate post-war world, and stories of Nazi Germany and of Hitler began to seep into our consciousness. We are a fortunate generation, for we came into this world just as the violence subsided, and we have enjoyed a lifetime of relative peacefulness. No bombs have fallen on us. We have not suffered invasion by foreign armies. In fact, we have on occasion been the invader. And now the fight is being brought back to us by incidents of terror on our own streets.

The cycle of violence is endless unless we do something to end it. Twenty-five years after the destruction of Pan Am Flight 103 over Lockerbie, a service of remembrance in Westminster Abbey heard wise voices speak for truth, for reconciliation and for peace. Dr Jim Swire, whose daughter Fleur died at Lockerbie, reminded us that the bombing of that flight had been a revenge attack. The Reverend John Mosey, who also lost a daughter, Helga, at Lockerbie, reminded us of the way of Jesus, and of the instruction of Saint Paul not to repay evil with evil but to overcome evil with good (see Romans 12:14-21).

In order for that to happen, we need to be born again. It is as if we need to begin our life again, and this time not to learn about cowboys and Indians, or if we do, not to be so readily persuaded that evil is all on the one side. The line between good and evil runs directly through the human heart, and we are all part of its problem.

When the Pharisee Nicodemus comes by night to talk to Jesus, there is so much that he wants to learn. He recognises in Jesus a man of God. Now he wants to learn all he can about the puzzle of life. In their conversation, Jesus utters mysterious words which in later days will become only too clear. He tells Nicodemus, 'The Son of Man must be lifted up as Moses lifted up the serpent in the desert, so that everyone who believes may have eternal life in him.'

In these words, Jesus gives us a glimpse into the very heart of God. How does God deal with us? How does God treat us? What kind of relationship did God create with us when he made this world? God has made us to be free human beings. God treats us with freedom, as his equals in relationship, and the only way that God wishes to rule over us is by loving us, not by over-lording us.

Nicodemus must wonder what this phrase 'lifted up' could possibly mean. Clearly people need to see God and to see God clearly if they are to follow him. When Jesus is taken out to Golgotha and nailed to a cross, the soldiers, using ropes, pull the cross upright and into its place. In that moment Nicodemus sees Jesus lifted up. Now he is up high in a prominent place for everyone to see. He even has a notice nailed up above his head: 'Jesus of Nazareth – The King of the Jews'.

In the moment of Jesus' death, Nicodemus brings precious ointment to anoint the body for burial. He knows, like the centurion guarding him knows, that this was a great and good man. Soon he will also know that this man will be truly lifted up, from the grave, and will be seen in glory. The figure of Christ on the cross will now blend in his mind with the risen Lord, alive and ascended to the living God. This is the exaltation.

At the Last Supper Jesus says to his friends, 'When I am lifted up from the earth, I will draw all men to myself' (John 12:32). Saint Paul, who was at first such a vigorous and energetic man and keen for the fray and the fight against evil where he saw it, came to understand a different way of fighting evil. All I know, he said, is Christ and him crucified (see 1 Corinthians 2:2). It is the mystery of suffering love that redeems the world, not violence: persevering love, not anger. Enduring love, not hatred.

The great divide is inside us, not outside. It is from the human heart that all evils things proceed, Jesus teaches us. Jesus was lifted up so that we could see him, and if we keep our eyes fixed on the crucified, our hearts may melt and our hearts will heal. A beautiful and ancient Lenten hymn, *Attende Domine*, implores the crucified Lord to have mercy on our sinful world:

> *Attende Domine, et miserere, quia peccavimus tibi.*
> 'Hear us, O Lord, and have mercy, because we have sinned against you.'

Fourth Monday of Lent
Blindness

Gospel: John 9:1-41

As long as I am in the world I am the light of the world.

David Lean's famous film *Doctor Zhivago*, being quite lengthy, had been given an interlude of 15 minutes the day I went to see it. We left the huddled refugees from the civil war in Russia crowded together in goods wagons, on a train hurtling east. When we returned to our seats and the cinema lights were turned low again, the film restarted with a black screen – the darkness of a tunnel – and the sound of the train trundling at speed over the tracks. We felt like those refugees all huddled together in those wagons.

Suddenly our eyes were struck by brilliant light as the train emerged from the darkness, and as they adjusted we saw the beauty of the Ural Mountains rising up in front of us, and then around about us the brilliant colours of the vast Russian steppe leading our eyes outwards for miles and miles to the horizon. Truly the world is a beautiful place, and how wonderful the gift of sight to behold it.

Those of us who can see, whose eyesight is good and healthy, quite simply take the gift of our sight for granted. It takes something like this contrast of darkness into light that David Lean conjured so brilliantly to make us stop and realise what a wonderful thing it is to be able to see.

A great game that children love to play is Blind Man's Bluff, where a child is blindfolded and has to try and catch other children without the aid of sight. If ever we are blindfolded, we realise how helpless we suddenly have become, how uncertain about anything and how dependent we are upon other people to be good to us and to guide us safely. When we can see, we think we know where we are going and we do not need the help of another.

All these things are in play on the day Jesus meets a blind man in the Temple in Jerusalem and gives to him the precious gift of sight. This simple act, this cure of the blind man, reveals so much about people. The man himself, overjoyed to be sighted, simply acknowledges that Jesus must be a good and holy man, blessed by God, to be able to do such a powerfully good thing.

But the religious authorities cannot see things quite so simply. For them, this healing is a threat to their own standing and position, and anyway the man who did this must be a charlatan, because he does not observe all the rules of the Sabbath. They refuse the simple evidence of their eyes and instead look for twisted interpretations of the facts.

These Jewish leaders send for the man who has been healed and try to interrogate him. They do not receive the answers they want and persist in their questioning until the man, in exasperation, asks if they intend to become followers of Jesus. They seem so interested in him! And these Jewish leaders fall back on the old defence. We rely on Moses, they say. We know he was from God. We know nothing about this man, Jesus. It is an appeal to ancient tradition and to the long since dead, to people they can claim for their own and to defend their position, while being dismissive of whatever they do not like in the modern world.

It is still a great line of defence in the Church for those who insist on the old ways and cannot tolerate anything new.

Jesus, in fact, is Alpha and Omega. He is of the old and of the new. His way is not a rejection of what went before, but the fulfilment of it. And he still is. In every age and in every generation, be it in society or in the community of the church, the Lord will bring old and new things into our lives. He wants to open our eyes and show us better and healthier ways in which to see things. But if we insist that we see already and that there is nothing new for us to learn, then we will be left in our blindness. And that will be our guilt. The Pharisee is in all of us.

The man who was cured said during his interrogation by the Pharisees, 'I only know that I was blind and now I can see.' This simple statement can serve as a motto and as an aim for all of us in life. There are so many things that we do not understand fully, if at all. It is good to realise that and to be able to admit it. We can then pray that the Lord will make paste and put it on our eyes to help us to see. It is when we think we know everything that we really are in trouble. Such an attitude will make us inflexible and rigid with regard to our ability to meet people and situations that we find difficult or problematic. Physical blindness is dark enough, but how deep is the darkness of those who are spiritually blind!

When we are spiritually blind we stumble around hurting ourselves and doing great damage to others. We only have to think of the game of Blind Man's Bluff to see how helpless people are when they cannot see the light. How grateful we can be then that the Lord has seen fit to put paste on our eyes and invite us to join the man born blind to wash each day in the Pool of Siloam.

What will my precious sight give me? The ability to see others in a kinder light? The ability not to judge others harshly? The ability to understand how little I know? Most of all, it may give me the grace to look on the face of Jesus and say with the blind man, 'Lord, I believe.'

> 'This I believe: I shall see the goodness of Yahweh, in the land of the living.' (Psalm 27:13)

Fourth Tuesday of Lent

Life

Gospel: John 5:1-3, 5-16

Get up, pick up your sleeping-mat and walk.

'Actions speak louder than words,' as an old saying has it, and indeed they do. When Jorge Mario Bergoglio was elected Pope in March 2013, he took the name Francis, after the saint of that name who lived a life of poverty as the expression of his love for God and all humankind. But taking such a name would not mean very much and would impress nobody very much if actions did not follow to demonstrate the sincerity and the genuineness of his intentions.

The new Pope then made the decision not to live in the papal apartment, but instead in more modest surroundings where he could have easier daily involvement with others. He needs community life; he does not like isolation.

Next the new Holy Father made his first trip outside Rome to the island of Lampedusa in the seas south of Italy, where desperate people, migrating from Africa, try to reach the shores of Europe and a better life. Many of these attempts end in the tragic failure of boats sinking and people – men, women and children – drowning. By going to this island, Pope Francis drew the attention, the eyes of the world, to this place, to this issue and to our need to be involved in the story of these poor people. The Holy Father has not ceased to do things on a personal level so that the watching world may see and come to appreciate the important messages that this Pope wants to convey to the community of this Earth.

When Jesus walked this Earth and began his public work, his actions were more powerful than his words, and his words were powerful enough! People need to see things happen before they will be impressed. We can all talk! So Jesus comes to Jerusalem and to the Sheep Pool, called Bethesda. This is a place where sick people gather. It is a healing pool of water, and whenever the water is disturbed, miracles of healing take place for the one who enters the pool first.

Among the many sick people gathered there, one man in particular is well known. He has been a regular at the pool for 38 years. It must be a case of every man for himself when the water starts to bubble, and this man, paralysed and with no assistant, is destined to spend his life there – until the Lord asks him if he wants to be well.

This question has always bemused me. Is it a case of simple politeness on the part of Jesus? You don't go around healing people who do not wish to be healed! Or did the question carry a deeper enquiry that perhaps the man was comfortable in his sickness? Just how much do you really want to be well? That is a powerful question to put to all of us at times. Does the question help to galvanise the man and to stir up in him a spirit for life, now that Jesus intends to make him well? So many different things happen in any human encounter and exchange.

'Get up, pick up your sleeping mat and walk.' This command of Jesus is very energising. Jesus does not bend down to help lift the man. No. This would be to hint that the man still needs help. He does not. The Lord has cured him completely. Not only can the man shift for himself, but he can also lift things and move by his own power. None of these things could he dream of doing before. He is completely well.

With this sign, this deed, Jesus shows the world who he is. As God is the giver of life and the healer of our ills, so now here, by this pool, Jesus shows us that God's power is working in him. He does God's deeds. The reaction of the authorities is to ignore the healing work, the good deed, and to find fault with the breaking of Sabbath regulations and local bye-laws. Jesus can only repeat in words what he has already said in deed. The Father does healing work and Jesus does the very same thing. Problem?

To the man who has been cured, when he meets him again, Jesus gives an important instruction. Illness and sickness are suffering enough. Make sure, now that you are well, that you do not use your good health for sinful purposes. The consequences of sin are far more serious than those of ill health.

In our own day we, too, can be exactly like the man beside the pool. Perhaps we feel sorry for ourselves, and if spiritual paralysis gets hold of us, we certainly do not lift a finger to help others. We might even indulge in the comfort of our sicknesses, not wanting to be well, not wanting to be any better than we are. In such a scenario, the Lord's question would be very necessary – do you want to be well?

The greatest sickness in life is spiritual, and the harm it does enormous. To be lazy, self-centred, insensitive to others, moody, angry and permanently disappointed with life – these are sicknesses of the soul that drag us down, and others with us. Very often people settle for the dismal condition in which they find themselves, they blame others for their woes, and they convince themselves that such is life. But the truth is far different from that.

A great Christian priest and writer, J.B. Phillips, spent fourteen years with the Greek text of the New Testament, as he made a new and popular translation. He was a man who suffered from depression, but his faith in the Lord helped him through. During his time of studying the Gospels in their original Greek he experienced a deep revelation about the Lord. The tremendous vitality of the person of Jesus seemed to rise from the page. Canon Phillips would later write about the human desire to understand life and to fathom the mystery of death. In Jesus, he tells us, we see what God is like, and we also discover that death is defeated.

Let us rise, take up our mat and walk.

'God, create a clean heart in me, put into me a new and constant spirit.' (Psalm 51:10)

Fourth Wednesday of Lent

Father and son

Gospel: John 5:17-30

The Son can do nothing by himself.

At Christmas time 2008 the writer Clive James wrote an article for *A Point of View* for the BBC. It was entitled, 'Lest We Forget, Jesus the Man'. It is a beautifully written piece in praise of the humanity of Jesus. As human thought from the time of the Renaissance moved away from the idea of the supernatural and the next life to concentrate on all that is natural and of this world, James writes to remind us, or to restate, what so many people think and feel – that Jesus is the most exemplary human being that there has ever been.

With the demise of his own personal faith, James goes on to say:

> I know that my redeemer liveth? Well I doubt if he can redeem me . . . But I do have faith that he lives on, as an ideal. All the Christian religions are lucky to have him, and those of us who have ceased to be Christians in the old way are lucky to have him too.[12]

At the end of the article James expresses his hope that we will be wise enough never to allow the memory of Jesus to die.

This sentiment that Clive James feels and expresses about the person of Jesus is a sentiment shared by many people. In a modern world that finds it hard or even impossible to

12. BBC News Magazine, 'Lest we forget, Jesus the man', 26 December 2008. Available at http://news.bbc.co.uk/1/hi/magazine/7799274.stm (accessed 12 April 2014).

believe in an afterlife, people are still affected by the person of Jesus. There is a respect for him and an acknowledgement of his beauty as a human being. People today, like people in Jesus' time, hold many and varied opinions about the man from Nazareth, but no one disputes his goodness or his humanity.

But if we listen more closely to the things Jesus says, we may learn more. When the Jews dispute with Jesus over his curing of a paralysed man, Jesus makes the claim that he does not act alone. He is not trying to stand out against the faith of Israel, but instead everything he says and does is at the behest of his 'Father'. Jesus is careful not to run ahead of himself. Sometimes we can say too much to people who are struggling to understand us and our behaviour. Word and action must keep pace with one another if we are to reveal something of our inner self to others.

Saint John, relating this story in his Gospel, written long after the time, expounds for us at greater length the inner world of Jesus that he has come to know in the course of his life. The God we cannot see, the world beyond that we do not know, is being gently revealed to us in the humanity of Jesus. The beauty that we see and that we praise as deeply human is also deeply divine. This is what Jesus is telling us. 'As the Father raises the dead and gives them life, so the Son gives life to anyone he chooses.'

For many people today, the idea of immortality is too much. Instead, they say that we live on in our children. Although this is not the meaning of personal immortality, something important is being said here. People are giving voice to the continuance of the spiritual life.

Only this morning, as I brought my coffee through to begin the day's work at my desk, I heard the voice of my father telling me to slow down. 'Take it easy now, Brian, there is no rush.' I smiled at the remembrance of a voice that has been silent these 25 years. Yet that voice lives in me spiritually, and the guidance that my father gave me long ago still comes through to guide me today. So there is a real sense in which we do live on in others, and especially in our children, for we are spiritual beings, and spiritual life flows into and through us all.

And the spirit does not die. People are sensing something of the divine when they speak of living on in their children, in the same way that people sense something beautiful in Jesus' humanity yet cannot name it fully. It is not possible to reveal yourself fully and completely in one word or one deed to another person. It takes time to get to know one another. Many words and many meetings must take place before we can grow into the lives of one another. Faith and trust in one another then lead us to love one another.

For Jesus it is the same. Scripture scholars refer to the 'Messianic Secret', to the fact that Jesus cannot simply say who he is as if it is a simple piece of factual information. Personal knowing is of a totally different order. Like the disciples, we begin as individuals or members of a crowd to hear about Jesus. Then we fall in step with him and become followers, and then we grow into disciples, and we never stop learning.

Today we hear Jesus referring constantly to his Father. Jesus is here to do his Father's will, not his own. If you accept the words of Jesus, then you have stepped into the realm of eternal life. Not only must we remember him, not only may he live in us, but we may now live in him. And to live in him is to know that we shall never die.

It is very poignant that the non-believer Clive James has produced a verse translation, in this last stage of his life, of Dante's great *Divine Comedy*. It is a task that he has given himself to do for many years. He dedicates the book to his wife, whose love he betrayed, but with whom there has been some kind of reconciling. 'We have broken bread together' is how James puts it.[13]

As life draws to a close for James, he is now deeply aware of the beauty of this world, just as he is also aware of the beauty of Jesus Christ. His non-believing eyes still see so much. How great is the vision granted to all who look upon the Lord and who can recognise in him the loveliness of the Father.

> 'For now we see in a mirror, dimly, but then we will see face to face.' (1 Corinthians 13:12)

13. Robert McCrum, 'Clive James – A Life in Writing', *Guardian*, 5 July 2013.

Fourth Thursday of Lent

Show me the evidence

Gospel: John 5:31-47

Besides, I know you too well: you have no love of God in you.

On Sunday afternoons when I was a child and my father was resting in the front room after his dinner, we four children used to persuade him to play Hunt the Thimble with us. It did not require too much effort on Daddy's part. He simply had to hide the thimble and then call us into the room, and as we searched he would tell us whether we were getting warm or getting cold as we neared or veered away from the hunted object. One Sunday afternoon he called us into the room to search, and try as we might, we could not find the thimble anywhere. We all came and stood around him and pleaded with him to tell us. 'Well, you are very warm now,' he said. With that clue we began to study our own father, and there, sitting among the strands of his hair, on top of his head was the thimble!

We could not find the thimble that day because we were looking in the wrong places, convinced that it was somewhere in the room – and it was. Yet the very place where the thimble was, we never considered to be a hiding place.

This memory came back to me as I read the words of Jesus as he speaks to the Jewish leaders about himself. 'You study the scriptures,' Jesus tells them, 'believing that in them you have eternal life; now these same scriptures testify to me, and yet you refuse to come to me for life!' The Jewish authorities are constantly asking Jesus to prove himself, to give some sign of who he is, to demonstrate clearly for all to see the truth about himself. This proof, or testimony or witness, is there in ample measure in the works of healing that Jesus does, but his opponents cannot and will not read the signs. They even quote Moses as someone they believe in, but as Jesus points out to them, Moses is useful to their purposes of holding power to themselves.

Then comes the withering critique of the Jewish leaders who oppose Jesus. You are not seekers after truth, Jesus tells them, and there is no love of God in you. Instead you live on human approval and on the passing mood of public opinion.

In our lives, the search for God, like Hunt the Thimble, requires our best efforts, yet God does not hide from us. All the evidence for God and God's love is revealed in Jesus himself. His words speak of God's truth and love. His healing works demonstrate the finger of God among us. His death and resurrection is the great sign of God's victory over all wickedness and over death itself. The difficulty lies with us. We often look in the wrong places, and we do not or cannot see what stands before our eyes.

Sometimes, trying to imagine what it would have been like to be there in the flesh during the time of Jesus, we may say that it would be impossible to accept the claims of Jesus to be a man sent by God. It is too enormous a thing to comprehend. Indeed, Jesus himself is only too aware of this issue. Revelation must come slowly and carefully. And so he points to the testimony of John the Baptist, who prepared the people for the imminent coming of someone special. He points to the healing works he does as witness to his genuine goodness. And he speaks openly for the whole world to hear. But that is not enough to save him from jealous criticism, from open hostility or from a cruel death.

In this passage of John's Gospel, Jesus points out that many a time we only seek the approval of one another for the things we say and do. We live on a moving horizontal plain. We seek to make our way in this world by learning the skills of social survival and social promotion. This is the criticism he levels at the religious leaders of the day. They live in a political and social environment in which the law of mutual approval is the fast track to a prosperous life. They are not particularly interested in justice and truth, except insofar as it might further their own purposes.

It reminds me of the infamous political pact made between Nazi Germany and Soviet Russia in 1941, between Ribbentrop and Molotov, when these parties agreed not to attack one another and so prepared the way for the total destruction of Poland. In a world made up of allies and enemies, the issues of justice and truth often take a back seat, or are completely ignored altogether.

In our social dealings with one another, we can too easily be swayed and influenced by a desire to be approved of rather than by the intention of acting with justice and honesty. The approval that really counts is the approval of our own conscience, that voice of God which lives within us. The conscience does not take sides. It is an inner voice that speaks for truth and justice. For believers, in addition to conscience, there is the person and the voice of the Lord to listen to every day. For all of us, believers and non-believers alike, there is the voice of conscience, and the honest counsel that we can seek from one another.

Just as an individual can be led astray by siren voices, so too can a whole nation and people. The example of what happened to the people of Germany at the time of Hitler is a warning from history to us all. The great voices in our own society can move public opinion into many strange alleys, and people feel social pressure to agree with the mood of the prevailing voices. It takes courage to swim against the tide.

Just as anxiety is not the way to live, neither is complacency. The word of God dwells among us and we can listen and learn every day of our lives. We can take the words of John's Gospel and say of God, 'We have heard his voice. We have seen his shape. His words find a home in us.'

> 'Yahweh, remember me for the love you bear your people.' (Psalm 106:4)

Fourth Friday of Lent

Knowing where we come from

Gospel: John 7:1-2, 10, 25-30

You know me and you know where I came from.

My mother came from a very poor part of Ireland, from County Mayo on Ireland's west coast. Her widowed mother brought up eight children on poor land in a poor cottage. I discovered that the old house was one long building and that the cows were kept in the end part, separated by a wall from where the people lived. They kept hens, geese and a pig. Water was brought from the river behind the house. Cooking was done on the turf fire. In later years I would talk to people about my mother's origins. 'You didn't tell them about the cows, did you?' she would ask me. She was not pleased to think that I would tell people about the level of poverty she knew. But for me, it was a proud boast that my mother and all her siblings came from such unpromising beginnings and went out into the wide world to become the people they were.

Later reflection brought to my mind the realisation that my father's childhood circumstances were in fact poorer than those of my mother. My father was born in industrial Lancashire in 1916, in a coalmining town, and the poverty of working-class people in those parts in those days was extreme. Cooped up in a narrow miner's house, living on the poor wages of a miner, who might sometimes work only two or three days a week when the mine owners slowed production, my father's childhood was far grimmer than that of my mother. Yet he, too, made his way in the world.

Our origins tend to brand us in people's minds. If our homes are poor, then perhaps we are no better. It is a regular mistake we make, to judge a book by its cover. No wonder now that book publishers take pains to produce attractive covers! When a certain Nathanael heard about Jesus and was told where he came from, his famous reply said it all: 'Can anything good come from that place?' (John 1:46).

We gather our impressions of people slowly, until on further acquaintance we feel we are getting to know them. Jesus is very aware of this, especially among the people of Jerusalem, the big city. In Galilee, Jesus is beginning to be something of a local hero – one of ours, who does good things. His reputation reflects glory on his fellow northerners. But down there in the south, in the capital, it is a different matter. Jesus does one work of healing and suddenly it is all over the papers, and everybody has their own opinion and view of the man.

When Jesus arrives in Jerusalem – quietly, so as not to stir up a fuss – the whispering is already in full flow, and he cannot remain anonymous for long. The great comment that is being made about his origins is, we know where he comes from! This is undisguised language for, 'This is a nobody!' Jesus could not be the Messiah, the 'One who is to come' (Matthew 11:3), because he does not fit the profile. Advance knowledge dictates that the Messiah will emerge mysteriously and no one will know his origins. So in the minds of many people Jesus is a non-starter.

Then Jesus responds to all this personal comment. Yes, you know where I come from, he says, but really you do not know me at all. Indeed, how little we really know about one another. The deeper truth about Jesus, which all this public opinion does not see, is that he comes from God, his Father.

Another truth about Jesus is that he has not just appeared suddenly. He was sent to us. He is a man on a mission.

In later days, when Jesus is arrested and brought before Pontius Pilate, he is questioned at length about his identity and his origins. Are you a king? What have you done? And finally, as Pilate grows exasperated, 'Where do you come from?' (see John 18:33-7; 19:9-11). This last question is an attempt to understand someone by going back to the beginning, to their origins. It is a natural thing to do. Not only does our place of origin have an influence on us, but the experiences of those early days are also formative of our personality and character. When we want to understand one another, this childhood information can be a revelation.

Where do I come from? It is a great question. Seeking information and answers to that question becomes important to us as the years go by. We find it interesting to learn about our forebears and the times they lived in. And from our immediate ancestors – our parents – comes so much that we can readily recognise about our own ways and temperament. But there is a deeper answer yet.

We come from the loving and creative hand of God. That is our true origin. Traces of the divine are in all of us. We are God's works of art. We are God's children. Scattered throughout the world, we are being called together into unity in Christ Jesus, each and every one of us. The gift of faith, given to us by God, has let us in on the secret. Now when we look at one another, even when we are strangers to one another in this world, we already know something very important about one another.

This knowledge and understanding is the daily gift of Christ Jesus to all who come to him. In our daily conversations with the Lord we will be given insight into the mystery of God, and wisdom in how to conduct ourselves in this world. Getting to know one another and getting to know the Lord is a lifelong journey. It is not a neat package; rather it is an ongoing adventure. Jesus teaches in the Temple daily and we must join him there and sit and listen to him, and even ask him questions such as, 'Who are you?' and 'Where do you come from?'

> 'They cry for help and Yahweh hears and rescues them from all their troubles.' (Psalm 34:17)

Fourth Saturday of Lent

Allegiances

Gospel: John 7:40-52

Would the Christ be from Galilee?

'The lamps are going out all over Europe; we shall not see them lit again in our lifetime.' Sir Edward Grey, the British Foreign Secretary, to whom this quote is attributed, was standing at a window in his office with a friend. Looking down on the street below, they watched as the evening lamps were being lit. That dusk in August 1914 was the immediate prelude to four years of horrendous warfare in Europe.

A hundred years on from those sad times, many scholars look back and study the minds and mentalities of all the players involved – princes, politicians and ordinary people – to see what dynamics were in play – military, emotional, psychological – and to see what lessons we may learn for ourselves in our own day with our own issues.

The same research needs to be done with every conflict that there has ever been so that we may learn something about ourselves and about our proclivity for warfare. The conflict may be international or about civil politics, about the ordering of society or about personal, human relationships. All are prey to the irruption of hostility and violence, and we have much to learn about ourselves.

One of the important factors in play at the time of the two great wars of the twentieth century was the matter of 'allegiances'. Nations made agreements with other nations for mutual support against other nations in the event of war breaking out. Such agreements, and the sense of duty in honouring them, made for a domino effect, one set of guns setting off the next. This so-called 'balance of power' as a method of keeping the peace failed miserably in the end. The League of Nations after the First World War and the United Nations after the Second World War have been moves away from allegiance to ongoing negotiation.

When Jesus comes to Jerusalem, he finds the issue of 'allegiances' very powerfully at work. The religious authorities do not like the idea of this young preacher from Nazareth and the north coming down to their patch – the important patch – and beginning to make a good impression on the locals. Rumours are beginning to spread that this Jesus is a very important person, and some of the things he is saying do not put the authorities in a very good light. It is a very clear-cut 'us and them' situation, and they know how to handle that: they send the police in.

But the police come back empty-handed. Not because they are frightened of making an arrest – though it might have been tricky – but actually because they are mightily impressed by Jesus themselves. Now, police are not the kind of people to be easily impressed by what people say. They have heard too much 'guff' for that. But here is a case of a genuine and favourable impression being made. Maybe they know the truth when they hear it.

The trouble with the authorities is that they are not prepared even to listen. Their minds are already made up. Their minds are closed to any persuasion. They take their stance first and come up with reasons afterwards . . . a very common human habit. They say to anyone who objects, 'Have you gone soft? Don't you know we are the experts in these matters? Are you from Galilee too? Whose side are you on?'

The authorities have cut to the chase. They are not interested in who Jesus is or what he has to say. What they know is that he is upsetting the apple cart, and with it their comfortable position and power. That, quite simply, must not be allowed to happen. If this man does not fall in line with their policies for society, they will have to deal with him. It is as simple as that.

In this story we see a mirror held up to ourselves and to our own behaviours. We live our lives by alliances and we form allegiances, and our first instinct is to protect our own whenever we feel they are being upset in any way. Sometimes our alliances are natural bonds of love and affection. Sometimes they are formed by traditional groups into which we have been born, and which manifest prejudice for and against others. Often our first question is not, 'Who are you?' Instead we ask, 'Whose side are you on?' When such differences have been a cause of bloodshed between people, feelings of hatred harden our hearts against any kind of acceptance of others.

The sufferings of all people in Northern Ireland offer us a lesson about ourselves, and about how hard it is to be free of prejudice when you have been hurt so much. Our experience of family life will also give us many lessons, showing how allegiance and loyalty to another may sometimes blind us to the greater issue of seeing justice done for all people.

The police who reported back about Jesus said a most eloquent and insightful thing about him: 'There has never been anybody who has spoken like him.' This is our salvation. Jesus is God's word spoken to us. To listen to the Lord every day of our life is to learn how to be a human being in this troubled world. The Lord will share with us, if we listen to him, all the wisdom of the ages, and all that we need for living life. His word is not simply information, but life-giving grace. It is a spiritual energy and dynamism for life.

Sit at the Lord's feet each day for a little while and listen to him. Let your heart be opened, and your mind, too. Let the Lord reveal to you your biases and your prejudices, your unfair judgements and your, sometimes cruel, opinions of others. Let the Word of God bring you to a place of fairness, where the air is fresh and where the view goes on forever. May the Lord set us free and help us make our way to Galilee.

'Yahweh my God, I take shelter in you.' (Psalm 7:1)

FIFTH WEEK OF LENT

Fifth Sunday of Lent
Life and death

Gospel: John 12:20-33

Now the hour has come.

When I was a child of seven or eight years old, I was taken to the pictures by my big cousin, Mike Walsh. Mike had spent the summer months working on farms in Lincolnshire, and now he was spending a few days with us before going home to Ireland. He was very keen to see a film called *Robin Hood*, and I asked if he would take me with him. The first 20 minutes or so of the film were fine enough, but suddenly, when the arrows began to fly and I heard the thud that they made as they plunged into human flesh, I became very frightened. There was no consoling me, so Mike, to his great irritation and frustration, had to come out of the cinema and take me home. I can feel to this day the disappointment oozing out of him as I apologised and walked beside him down the road. The last time I ever spoke to Mike, in his old age, was in a phone call shortly before he died. 'Hello Brian,' he said, 'this is Robin Hood speaking.'

That visit to the cinema was the occasion of my first ever confrontation with violence. It was very frightening to a young child. At home I might play Cowboys and Indians and pretend to shoot bullets or arrows at others, but sitting in a darkened cinema with my eyes focused on the full-colour images of blood, pain and death was too much to bear. Many years later, when I was 20, another visit to a cinema – this time to see a war film – was the occasion of a fainting fit when I saw a needle being ripped out of a patient's arm. I am a sensitive child!

Violence and cruelty happen every day in this world. People inflict terrible hurts and atrocities on others. Not just some people, but all of us. It is a shock to my system to say it, but if my country is involved in warfare, then I am part of what my country does, and to the victim, long-range killing is not really different from close-up killing. Acts of cruelty are carried out every day. Children are neglected or abused. Adults argue and fight. People assault one another. Verbal viciousness abounds. Hatred grows in the soul. Many people find themselves caught in the middle of violent outbreaks, and their lives are terribly damaged as a result, and all they want is to live in peace. And peace does not come. Instead their lives are marked by the two great evils – sin and death.

In the Gospel today, Jesus talks about his own coming confrontation with these evils, and describes it as the moment of his glorification. His 'hour' is upon him. He speaks in guarded language to his disciples; he does not wish to alarm them. Coming events will do that soon enough. Jesus has no wish to die, or to suffer in any way. But the forces of evil are hunting him. He could try to escape, but to do that he would have to deny his own self – to stop being, to stop saying, to stop doing. 'Life with death contended', as the Easter hymn will say.[14] We must stand up in life or forever cower in the corner.

In the Passion story of Jesus we see a man who stands up, and stands up straight. When the soldiers come to

14. The Easter Sequence, *Victimae paschali laudes,* in the Mass of Easter Day.

Gethsemane to arrest him, he stands up straight before them and they cower; they fall back. In the house of the High Priest, and again before Pilate, Jesus stands up straight. He confronts the evil that assaults him (John 18). He knows he will not be shamed, even as he is abused and mistreated. And on the cross, lifted high, this loveliest of human beings is not cowed. His cross is the throne of a king. His suffering the price he will pay for love. His death an act of trust in his heavenly Father who will not abandon him forever.

This is how an atrocity has become a glory: love has triumphed over hatred. The price paid is in suffering, but the reward is our hope of glory too. The death and resurrection of Jesus has now become our 'way of life'. This triumphant road is the road we are asked to walk, as followers in his footsteps. In particular, Jesus says that wherever he is in this world, there his servant will be also. This means that wherever there is suffering in this world, we must play our part. Like the Lord himself, we are asked to stand up straight and to face the 'hour' that comes to us, and to share in the sufferings of others.

As the disciples came to understand Jesus and his story, they began to preach it and to try and live it. Saint Paul, that energetic, not to say violent, individual, came to see that the way to follow is not to repay evil with evil, but to repay it with good (see Romans 12:17). Saint Peter, who could not tolerate the idea that Jesus would allow himself to suffer, came round to saying that we should consider it an honour if we have to suffer for bearing the name of Christ (1 Peter 4:14-17). These men and women, the early followers of the Lord, were not cowards. For each one of them the 'hour' of suffering would come, and they would face it. For they now knew that love is stronger than death, and that in the battle between life and death, the combat was strangely ended. 'Life own champion slain, yet lives to reign.'[15]

Jesus turns our attention to the grain of wheat which, left to itself, simply does nothing. But if it is buried in the ground, it bursts forth into new life – an abundance of life. Our lives, too, if we live them in love for one another, will produce a harvest of blessing. Our life is our 'hour'.

> 'Be my saviour again, renew my joy, keep my spirit steady and willing.' (Psalm 51:12)

15. The Easter Sequence, *Victimae paschali laudes.*

Fifth Monday of Lent

Jesus wept

Gospel: John 11:1-45

I am the resurrection and the life.

The small town of Newport in the County of Mayo, on Ireland's west coast, boasts an impressive Hiberno-Romanesque Church with a particularly striking doorway. The church sits high above the town and looks down on the magnificent arched viaduct that once carried a railway line to Achill Island. If the outside of the church is impressive, the inside is equally striking in its simple stone purity of style. At the far end, overlooking the sanctuary, is a beautiful stained glass window, depicting the Last Judgement. This window is the work of a famed Irish artist, Harry Clarke, and his school.

In June 2013 I made a pilgrimage to this church, in the aftermath of my wife's sudden death, and I stood before this beautiful window and felt the atmosphere of a holy place. I was in the days of sorrow for the loss of Margaret, my wife, and grateful for the peace and tranquillity of this church. As I stood there before the altar rails, my eyes were drawn to my left, and I saw in a small window the yellow and white colours of another stained glass, and in this window the words looking back at me, 'I am the resurrection and the life.'

Suddenly I was in tears. Easy, gentle tears began to stream down my face as I thought of Maggie and heard the words of the Lord addressed to me. There, in that moment, I grieved and I rejoiced in the truth I have come to know – Jesus is Lord and is risen from the dead.

Feelings such as these abounded in the days when Lazarus, the friend of Jesus, died. Martha and Mary, the sisters of Lazarus, are in mourning, and Jesus weeps too when he meets with them. Often when we cry, we cry for more reasons than we know. One sorrow can touch another, buried deep inside us, and our crying for one can trigger crying for another. The tears that Jesus sheds for Lazarus could also involve tears for the people who would not accept him, and tears for his coming suffering and death. Jesus knows what lies ahead of him. Even as he is about to work a great wonder and raise Lazarus to life, he knows that very soon he himself will be put to death. No wonder Jesus weeps.

Some instinct in Mary, the sister of Lazarus, led her to anoint the feet of Jesus with precious ointment, and to wipe his feet with her hair. She is doing this for the day of my burial, Jesus explained, when Judas objected. Somehow she knew that Jesus was going to run into trouble. He was, indeed, too good for this world. Intriguingly, many years before, the Greek philosopher Plato had asked the question, 'What would happen to a man who was perfectly just and honourable in this world?' His answer? 'That man would be crucified!'

The tears we shed are expressions of love for someone or something that we have lost. They are healing waters. Through our tears we express love; we feel close to the one we have lost. We cry our sadness out of our body literally. Sometimes the person we cry for is ourself, and our tears are for a life not lived as it could have been, for chances missed, for a road not taken, for joy that did not come. When our tears do not flow, it can be because we have dammed them up for fear that we might be drowned in them. Some pains are so deep and some hurts so raw that we block access to them, attempting to avoid the pain and the flood of tears that we fear might wash us away.

When Jesus comes to carry his cross through the streets of Jerusalem, he meets with some women who are crying in pity for his plight. 'Do not weep for me,' says Jesus; 'weep rather for yourselves and for your children' (Luke 23:28). Jesus knows the suffering that will come down upon these poor people, because people will not listen (see Luke 19:41-4).

Our world is full of heartbreak and unshed tears; of people not listening to one another; of people not hearing what another is trying to say; of people with hearts hardened against others; of people who have suffered too long and too silently. There are many reasons why we cry. 'If you have tears prepare to shed them now,'[16] for a suffering world torn by warfare, for a suffering society torn by injustice, for suffering people torn apart by anger and betrayal.

In the face of this sorrow and sadness, Jesus looks into the eyes of Martha and says to her, 'I am the resurrection and the life . . . Do you believe this?'

'Yes Lord,' says Martha. 'I believe that you are the Christ, the Son of God, the one who was to come into this world.'

Now we have our answer. Now we have our reason for tears. Tears of joy that the Lord is with us, and the Lord will hear us. Let the tears flow. Do not allow this world and its sufferings to harden your heart. The Book of Revelation says of God, 'He will wipe away all tears from their eyes' (Revelation 21:4). That is what love does, and what God wishes to do.

On the day I visited Newport and its splendid church, I travelled further on and came to the sea at Mulranny. This

---

16. William Shakespeare, *Julius Caesar*, Act 3, scene 2.

was a favourite beach for family holidays, and now, without Margaret, I suddenly burst into great sobs. My brother held me while I cried. Later that day, and further down the road of travel, on a sun-blest beach in Belmullet, I stood on the edge of the sea and lifted my eyes and my arms to the sky, and I smiled for joy at the thought of my beloved wife now in heaven. There were no tears on that beach. The Lord had wiped them away.

> 'For me the reward of virtue is to see your face, and, on waking, to gaze my fill on your likeness.' (Psalm 17:15)

Fifth Tuesday of Lent
Resistance

Gospel: John 8:21-30

You will look for me and you will die in your sin.

Many years ago I happened to visit the ancient church of Saint Martin in the village of Cheriton that overlooks the English Channel at Folkestone. What I did not know at the time is that there, buried in the churchyard, lies the body of one Samuel Plimsoll. This man was responsible for waging a campaign through Parliament for better conditions for sailors at sea – to save them from working on the 'coffin ships' by bringing in regulations for the improvement of ships and a limit on cargo carrying. His ultimate success saw the introduction of the 'Plimsoll line' – a line along a ship's hull indicating the maximum safe draft for all ships at sea.

In earlier days, Samuel Plimsoll had fallen on hard times in business, and he lived for a while in a common lodging house. He saw and experienced at first hand the plight of the poor, and when his circumstances improved, Plimsoll resolved never to forget the experience and to work for the betterment of conditions for the poor. At that time the lot of sailors was a precarious one: they worked on ships that were not seaworthy, often overloaded and heavily insured by their owners. Sailors' lives were always at risk.

When Plimsoll set out to change this situation and to move Parliament to do something, he came up against great opposition and resistance from fellow Members of Parliament – for the simple reason that many of them were also ship owners! Such is our human condition! We do not stand in the way of change as long as it does not affect us or our interests in any way. If we stand to lose anything as a result of change, we dig our heels in!

This story is a great lesson to us all. Human self-interest – not to say greed – often stands in the way of justice and puts up stubborn resistance to any change that seems to threaten our own prosperity. The issue of 'Nimby' – not in my back yard – challenges us all.

When Jesus comes to prominence among the Jews, his presence and his preaching is clearly a challenge to them. Jesus knows that people will have difficulty in absorbing him and his teaching, and he is careful not to make outlandish statements about himself. He never calls himself the 'Messiah'. Titles and slogans cause more trouble than they are worth. Jesus has not come to disrupt life – that is not his purpose – or to overturn the Law. I have come to fulfil the Law, he says (see Matthew 5:17-19).

Jesus speaks openly for all the world to hear, as he will later remind the High Priest at his interrogation (John 18:20). He will also let his works of healing speak for themselves. Nobody could do the things you do if they did not come from God. So said the man who was cured of his blindness (John 9:30-3). So, too, said Nicodemus when he came to Jesus by night (John 3:1-2). For which of these works are you stoning me, asked Jesus, when he was threatened (John 10:31-2). Jesus communicates himself to us in the most human of human ways. And still people hesitate to accept him. Worse than this, those in positions of power, those who feel they have much to lose, decide to do away with Jesus. He can hardly be called a troublemaker, but he is causing trouble for them!

We see here at work, once more, the resistant forces of self-interest and greed. Someone has appeared who threatens the firmly established status quo, and this person must be stopped. It brings to mind the person and the figure of Gandhi in India, and the film that so brilliantly portrayed his life, made by Richard Attenborough. It was a British official in India in 1918 who pointed out that it is very difficult to fight against an opponent who has no self-interest in the argument, but who is purely concerned with matters of justice and fairness for all. Appealing to self-interest can give us some leverage in a contest, but where there is none, where selflessness is before us, we are at a loss. Then either we resort to force and violence, or we must change!

In all his discussions with the Pharisees, Jesus explains that he is not acting purely on his own authority, but that he teaches what he has learned from his Father. Even in saying this, he is not outlandish, and on one occasion he questions, as we are all God's children, what is wrong in what he says? There is no justification for what happens to Jesus – none whatsoever. He comes among us in human simplicity and openness, and he is crucified for it. He is not the first, and he won't be the last.

There is opportunity for great examination of conscience for us here. Self-interest is a natural part of our make-up. We have powerful loyalties in bonds of blood and friendship. But often those bonds can tie us up and make us resistant to change, unwilling to consider other people and their points of view. And self-interest can very easily descend into greed and into concern for our own well-being, no matter what the cost might be to others in matters of justice and fairness.

In the end, when all talking is done, Jesus is taken out and led away to be crucified. It is then, when he hangs upon the cross, that people can see that here is a man who gave himself to us completely, a man who made of his life a self-sacrifice for love of us, a man who is obedient to his heavenly Father unto the moment of his death. This cross of Christ has been lifted up in the world ever since that fateful day, and people have looked upon it and have studied the man who is nailed there, and have come to see in this Jesus the saviour of the world.

It is at this time that the Roman centurion, who stands beneath the cross and watches the spectacle and the way Jesus dies, gives his witness to the crucified: 'This was a great and good man' (Luke 23:47).

'I am the light of the world,' says the Lord. (John 8:12)

Fifth Wednesday of Lent

Truth and freedom

Gospel: John 8:31-42

You will learn the truth.

I remember as a child going to Mass in our little parish church in Lancashire. The church is closed now, but it is still standing, saved by a preservation order, although it is still subject to the forces of the weather. And the district in which it stands has also changed. The church was built and stood in Lancashire for most of its life, but it now stands in Greater Manchester.

In my childhood days, when Mass was murmured in Latin, the priest would stand at the left side of the altar to recite the Gospel in the holy mutter. Then he would come away from the sanctuary, climb into the fine, wooden pulpit at the left side of the church, stare down at the assembled congregation and give out notices and then the sermon.

The two locations, altar and pulpit, now seem to me to signify the fault line between the gospel as taught by Jesus and the gospel as relayed to us by a priest. In our hands, as in our lives, the beautiful truth of the gospel can become a very sullied and uncertain thing, a narrow vision and an unfaithful rendering of God's word. Hence the fragmentation of Christianity into so many different churches and branches.

In those 1950s days of my childhood, I remember a fine-looking church just up the road from my Catholic chapel, but it was a Church of England. I was a Catholic boy of Irish descent growing up in Protestant England, and going inside a Protestant church in those days and attending a Protestant service was deemed to be a serious sin! This was a very confusing state of affairs for a young child – to hear the words of Jesus about love of neighbour and at the same time to be told that Protestants were not quite right. Somewhere between the altar and the pulpit the gospel of Jesus was being betrayed.

Since those far-off days, the churches have reached far better and kinder understandings of one another. Today our uncertain look is cast not at fellow Christians but at a public media world in which religion itself is regarded as doubtful at best and downright intolerable at worst. A particular problem that the world has with the Church is over the issue of 'truth'.

Pilate famously utters the comment, 'Truth? . . . What is that?' (John 18:38). In his struggle to deal with a crowd that is baying for blood at the trial of Jesus, persuasion is one of his tactics, and practical politics his ultimate solution, but the truth he regards as being of no help at all. And, understandably, in a world that does not 'do God', claims to know the truth are regarded as outrageous attempts to bully others into a particular viewpoint. Our modern world moves forward according to political consensus and according to majority vote interpretations. Truth is just too hard a concept to handle.

And yet Jesus speaks about truth as being the most important thing in life. His words are instructive. Listen to his word. Make that word your home. In other words, live in it. If you do so you will be my disciples – that is, people who learn things, and you will learn what the truth of life is and then you will experience freedom.

These words of Jesus tell us so much. Truth is not something we can ever possess. Instead we can enter into its greatness, like walking into a building. The truth we will come to know will change us into loving and tolerant people. Truth is not something that divides people; rather, it brings them together. God is love and God is truth. To enter into the spirit of God is to come close to one another.

The first challenge that truth makes will be to ourselves and to our ways of looking at the world. There is a saying, attributed to James Garfield (1831–1881), the assassinated US President, which tells us that, 'The truth will make you free, but first it will make you miserable.' Yes, the truth will first of all show to us our own sinfulness and our weaknesses, our prejudices and our narrow ways. But this is not a negative thing; it is a purifying grace.

Having cleansed us of narrow and negative attitudes, the grace of Christ's truth is to lead us in the path of love for one another. Such a journey will involve learning about other people, their stories and their ways of life, their values and their gifts. Tolerance and acceptance of others is the grace that comes from learning the truth of Christ Jesus. There is so much for us to learn!

In the great forum of public argument and debate, it is understandable how many people are wary of religion. In our history there have been many episodes of intolerant and narrow attitudes at work, harming the lives of others. It is no wonder some people will not even listen to religious language any more.

But that is not the end of it. We all share a common language, and this language is our human nature and human experiences. In studying together this nature of ours, we may come to discover the truth about ourselves. The humanist and the Christian can speak a common language as we search for what is good, just, loving and true in our shared life.

Our understandings and our observations are things to be offered to one another, not things to be hurled at one another. In the present issue of euthanasia, for example, our common feeling is one of compassion for all who suffer, and the differing solutions that we propose are compassionate resolves. And we see the end of life's meaning differently. It is important to acknowledge all the goodness on both sides of this argument.

No matter what our problems and difficulties with each other might be, the words of Jesus hold true for us. 'If God were your father, you would love me.' That is how we must be towards all. For love is the greatest truth of all.

> 'As for the part in the rich soil, this is people with a noble and generous heart who have heard the word and take it to themselves and yield a harvest through their perseverance.' (Luke 8:15)

Fifth Thursday of Lent
Someone who knows God

Gospel: John 8:51-59

At this they picked up stones to throw at him.

I had an uncle called Patrick, but I never knew him. He died when he was only seven years old. Some boys were throwing stones and Patrick was hit on the head. He went home complaining of a headache, and a few days later he died. This happened around 1919. My father would have been just three years old. I know nothing more about this incident, and nothing more about Patrick. His short life was ended. For his mother, my grandmother, it was all part of a very sad time. She had already lost two of her brothers in the Great War – John in Flanders in May 1916, and Owen in Mesopotamia at Christmas 1917. Now, just two years later, one of her children was taken from her as well.

Stone throwing, bullet firing, bomb dropping: it is all the same thing – acts of violence against our fellow creatures of flesh and blood. We still do it, everywhere and all the time – violent reactions to offences real or imagined. It is a form of language, but it is of the worst kind, guaranteed not to communicate but to condemn and crucify others. It often begins with language and with conversation, which then becomes intolerable language, from which people are able to walk away. But then, having given up on words, people pick up stones.

This happens to Jesus on more than one occasion. In his home town of Nazareth, the people turn against him and threaten his life because of things he says. In Jerusalem, in conversation with the Pharisees, he is threatened with stones because he claims to come from God. People sometimes become very angry at the things we say. All violence begins with words, for words carry the intentions of the heart, and as Jesus taught us, all evil desires begin in the human heart (Mark 7:21).

It seems important therefore, in our efforts to bring an end to violence, that we start where the trouble begins – with our own hearts. It is there, in the silence and privacy of the human heart, that we hold our daily conversations. We think good thoughts or we harbour grievances and resentments. These hearts of ours will be peaceable places or troubled places, according to the experiences of our lives – in particular, whether we have been loved or mistreated, cared for or neglected.

In her autobiography, *Why Be Happy When You Could Be Normal?* Jeanette Winterson speaks about her adoptive father who in old age suffered an outburst of violence and threw crockery around the house. Jeanette took her dad up the Lancashire hills and after some silence they talked. Her father began to tell her about his D-Day experience: having no gun, but only a bayonet, he killed six men. He spoke of coming home to Liverpool and going to sleep in an empty house, and waking up to find that the house lay in ruins after a bombing raid. He had slept through it. His childhood had been a neglected one and his first marriage a time of massive repression at the hands of a religiously unbalanced wife.

Jeanette reflects on this man, her father, saying:

> He was always a little boy, and I am upset that I didn't look after him, upset that there are so many kids who

> never get looked after, and so they can't grow up. They can get older, but they can't grow up. That takes love. If you are lucky the love will come later. If you are lucky you won't hit love in the face.[17]

The first great battlefield of life is the human heart, not any desert sand, beachhead or ocean wave. The hurts done to the heart by the heart of another is our battleground. The secret and sacred centre of every person is the place we must protect and safeguard from harm. And when heart speaks to heart we can say that we really are coming to know someone. Until then we can know about one another, our shape and our size, but when we begin to know the ways of a person from what they say and how they behave, we begin to learn what is in the heart. Body language is a gateway into the soul.

Many religious people know a great deal *about* God, but as for actually *knowing* God, they can be completely ignorant. To know God we must listen with the heart to what God says to the heart. If we do not hold any conversations with God, how can we ever claim to know him?

It is our great good fortune to know about Jesus Christ, the Son of God. Now we have the opportunity to come to know God truly through coming to know the Lord. And the first thing we can say is that anyone who is wilfully violent in any way does not know God. The example we have learned from the Lord is of grace and the virtue of patient suffering. This is the meaning of his cross – that we be prepared to suffer one another and not to offend or harm one another in any way.

17. Jeanette Winterson, *Why Be Happy When You Could Be Normal?* Jonathan Cape, London, 2011, p.49.

Each day we go out into the world. Each day we meet and talk with others. Our words affect everyone we speak with, for those words carry love, indifference, coldness or hurt to another. Our words can be expressions of affection, justice and honesty, or they can be volleys of abuse and aggressive hostility. Like stones, our words can be used to build sheltering homes for people, or they can be used as projectiles for the purpose of hurting others.

Sometimes a careless word can cause great hurt, just like a careless stone thrown long ago hit my uncle Patrick and caused first a headache and then death. It is time for us to learn to know the Lord.

> 'Seek Yahweh and his strength, seek his face untiringly.'
> (Psalm 105:4)

Fifth Friday of Lent
May I speak?

Gospel: John 10:31-42

At least believe in the work I do.

During an oppressed and unhappy childhood, the writer Jeanette Winterson lived with an adoptive mother who refused to have any books in the house. 'You never know what's in them until it's too late,' her mother would say. Jeanette used to secrete books into the house and hide them under her mattress. But one day her mother spotted a book that was not properly hidden away, and she overturned the mattress and found 70 more! They were all taken out to the back yard, had paraffin poured over them and were set alight.[18] Jeanette's mother had a terrible fear of the world. To her it was a wicked place, and its evil influences had to be stopped. Projecting her own unhappy feelings and complexes on to her husband and her adopted daughter, Mrs Winterson lived in a dark and miserable world. Jeanette, on the other hand, was determined to find the light in her life; she continued to read and began also to write.

A similarly fearful attitude is evident and in play in the Jewish leaders who oppose Jesus. They feel their controlled world to be threatened by this man who comes preaching the love of God and doing works of healing. The works they cannot deny, but the words of Jesus they can object to. They are determined not to allow his version of truth, his words of interpretation, to rival to their own. He must be stopped. He

18. Winterson, *Why Be Happy When You Could Be Normal?*, chapter 3, pp.33-43.

must be prevented from speaking and from saying things that they cannot cope with, things that might alter or change in any way the manner in which their own world is ordered.

This is the way with any kind of dictator. 'My way or no way' is their creed, and all other versions of the story must be banished and their books burned. It has happened throughout the course of history. Oppression begins with the burning of books and the shutting up of opponents. Dictators do not want people to think thoughts other than the ones they approve of. Knowledge is power, and power can be dangerous. In recent history we often see film coverage of the burning of books at the time of the rise of Adolf Hitler to power in Germany. And the world is full of 'little Hitlers'.

In ordinary domestic life, in families growing up together, freedom of speech is not always allowed. People in their own homes can be tyrants, ruling with harshness and cruelty over the other members of the household. Certain things cannot be spoken about. Certain things cannot be said. And holding a different opinion on a subject can cause a person to be thrown out of the house. Domestic violence is often the unseen and untold story. Unhappy, insecure and tormented people can rule in their own homes like the cruellest of tyrants. Nobody knows about it, and it can go on for years.

Jeanette Winterson had the courage, the bravery and the fierce determination to leave home and to escape from her oppressive environment. In the story of Jesus and his oppressive opponents in Jerusalem, we are told that Jesus escapes too. He leaves the city and goes to stay on the far side of the Jordan River, away from the heat of verbal condemnation, away from the threat of being stoned as a blasphemer, away from the narrow-minded religion that so opposes him.

In our own world, many people cannot or do not escape from their oppressive surroundings. For a multitude of reasons – among them fear and lack of confidence, as well as the perceived lack of an alternative – many people stay in the same house with an abusive partner. They cower in the face of oppressive, cruel and vindictive people, and the person inside is crushed; the voice that God gives them is not heard.

Every human person is a beautiful expression of the divine image if it is allowed to grow and to flourish. Every human voice deserves to be heard, to speak and to say who they are, and to sing. Yes, to sing. The story of people picking up stones to throw at Jesus is testimony to how blind we can become to the loveliness of one another in this world. Some people we do not recognise as beautiful at all. Some people do not know themselves to have any beauty to admire or celebrate. And all around us people pick up stones, literally and metaphorically, to throw at others. The words of Jesus ring out loud and clear: for what good reasons are you about to stone this person?

In a famous situation when people are about to stone a woman for the act of adultery, Jesus gives them their cue: let the person who is without sin cast the first stone (John 8:3-7). We should not pick up stones, nor encourage others to do so. None of us are without fault.

The ways of peace are dearly bought ways. The price we must pay is a price that involves our patience and our suffering. If we will join ourselves to the Spirit of the Lord and walk in his way, then the way of the cross is the path we are invited to walk. In personal life, in social life, in the life of international relationships, the road to peace is a road that demands our patience and our perseverance. In his first message for peace at New Year 2014, Pope Francis highlighted the virtue of fraternity, the brotherly and sisterly attitude that comes from knowing that we are all of the one family. This is a quality of understanding so precious and inspirational.

Looking back at her own harsh upbringing, the adult Jeanette Winterson could commiserate with the woman who had caused her so much misery. Jeanette had learned wisdom from her sufferings and gained an insight into the woman she called her mother. 'She was such a solitary woman,' Jeanette writes. 'A solitary woman who longed for one person to know her. I think I do know her now, but it is too late.'[19]

> 'Hard-pressed, I invoked Yahweh, he heard me and came to my relief.' (Psalm 118:5)

19. Winterson, *Why Be Happy When You Could Be Normal?*, pp.57-8.

Fifth Saturday of Lent

Eyes to see

Gospel: John 11:45-56

From that day they were determined to kill him.

At a luncheon in the American White House on 26 June 1954, the British statesman Winston Churchill made the comment that was later reported as, 'It is better to jaw-jaw than to war-war.'[20] This is quite a remarkable comment, coming as it did from a man who was born into a military dynasty – he was descended from the Marlborough family – and who fought in the Sudan as a young man, in South Africa during the Boer War and in the trenches during the First World War, and who led Britain into the sustained war against Nazi Germany in the 1940s. Churchill had been called a warmonger in the 1930s because of his warnings about the rise of Hitler and the corresponding need for Britain to arm itself for defence.

In the years that have passed since those terrible days, the narrative of bravery, heroism and self-sacrifice that marked the lives of British people has been the dominant narrative in our lives and in the retelling of those stories. In years to come, when this generation has passed away, perhaps other questions will be asked about the choices and decisions that were made. So many millions of people died in that terrible conflict that it is important to ask awkward and unpopular

---

20. Attributed to Winston Churchill at a luncheon in the White House, 26 June 1954, and reported in the *New York Times*, 27 June 1954.

questions, not simply to retell the story, but to interrogate the narrative and so to learn for ourselves the wise way to proceed, in our turn, when faced with the threat of war.

Peace not war. Issues of justice and of peace, issues of fairness and equality, issues of cooperation and solidarity never go away. In each new generation the task of caring for one and for all remains paramount. Every year on 1 January the Holy Father issues a message on the subject of peace. Each year our minds and hearts are directed to consider particular aspects of this great cause and how we might establish the ways of peace in our world.

This same task faces the religious and political leaders of Jerusalem at the time of Jesus. In fact, Jesus is the issue that is causing them great alarm. His rising profile and popularity are giving cause for concern to the elders and chief priests of the time. They become alarmed that his profile could start a movement of national independence, which in turn would bring down the wrath of the Roman Governor upon them. They fear that they might lose everything. The Temple, the city and the country itself could be lost if something is not done.

A meeting is held and the whole matter discussed. When all their fears have been voiced and the people are searching for a policy solution to the present danger, the leader of the Jews, the High Priest Caiaphas, makes his telling intervention. You are not looking at this properly, he says. The answer is a simple one: get rid of the troublemaker and the trouble will go away. Sacrifice this one man and the general population will be saved. It really is quite simple. Perhaps a sigh goes round the room. Thank God for decisive leadership! The meeting ends with a resolution that Jesus must be apprehended and done away with.

As things turn out, the very fears that drive those leaders to kill Jesus come back to haunt the Jews, and within a generation the Temple is destroyed and the Jewish nation scattered.

Looking at this narrative today, and indeed looking at all narratives of conflict, we can call to our aid the particular message for peace that Pope Francis issued in January 2014. At the very beginning of that message, the Holy Father said that if we are aware of the relatedness of human beings to one another, then we may come to see that in truth we are brothers and sisters to one another in one human family.[21] We may come to see that another person is a brother, a sister, and not a rival. Our problems are always shaped and defined by the way we see them, by our perception and our interpretation of them.

Realistically, we know that our human brokenness is the cause of our trouble. The story of Cain and Abel in Genesis 4 highlights for us the difficulties we find with one another – the jealousy, the selfishness and the greed. But the death of Jesus and his resurrection has taken our humanity through the gates of wickedness and destruction and brought us into a new life in the risen Lord. It is in this grace and by this power that we can see with new eyes the truth of our family ties and of our real togetherness as brothers and sisters.

Now, with these new eyes and this fresh understanding, the followers of the Lord can work every day for the peace of this world. The risen Lord calls us to live in him and to be part of the great work of bringing together the scattered children of God. This work begins with our own selves, as all good things must. Pope Francis brings our attention to the excessive lifestyles that we in the developed world are

21. Pope Francis, Message for World Day of Peace, 1 January 2014, section 1, paragraph 2.

constantly being encouraged to follow. The world we inhabit and think of as normal is in fact a world dominated by voices that encourage our luxury and our greed. When I become aware of that truth, I must respond and simplify my life.

As the Jewish leaders determine to kill Jesus and Jesus himself withdraws from the city and from its dangers, the feast of the Passover draws near. That feast commemorates and celebrates the great escape from Egypt and from oppression. It is a feast of freedom. When Jesus dies on the cross and becomes our new Passover lamb, he brings us into a greater freedom – the freedom of the sons and daughters of God. This is the world we are called to live in. It is a new world, and in it each day we may live and work in the Lord to bring together in unity the scattered children of God.

> 'He who scattered Israel gathers him, he guards him as a shepherd guards his flock.' (Jeremiah 31:10)

HOLY WEEK

Palm Sunday
A donkey ride

Gospel: Mark 11:1-10

When they were approaching Jerusalem.

I have in my possession a photograph taken on holiday in the west of Ireland when I was about nine years old. It is mid morning and I am leaning against my father's shoulder as he sits on a grassy bank. My father was a coalminer and I loved him, and it was wonderful as a child just to be in physical contact with him. We are in my mother's home place and Mum took the photograph. As we smile towards the camera, there in the background is a donkey. Tethered by its hind leg to keep it safely stationed, the donkey is stretching as far as it can to reach for juicy grass. In those happy, far-off days of childhood holidays, I often recall the trips we made to the bog to collect turf for the fire, and how our donkey walked so steadily and quietly up and down the 'boreen'. They are such gentle, quiet, humble animals. You just have to love them.

In our Lord's life, as he reaches the days of his arrest, trial and condemnation, a donkey comes into the picture. Some quiet, gentle animal – a young foal that has never been ridden before – is brought along for Jesus to sit on and to ride in triumph into the holy city of Jerusalem. There has been a growing feeling of expectation among the people, just as there has been a growing animosity between the young preacher and the authorities. Jesus has spoken in the Temple.

He has performed works of healing, and still he is regarded as unacceptable – dangerous, even. So now, when all words are spoken and all good deeds done, it only remains for a sign to be given, a symbolic act to let people see truly how things are. Jesus will enter the holy city as its king. This is a deliberate act by Jesus to let the world see and know that he truly is a king.

His chosen animal – a humble donkey, a beast of burden – will carry him into the streets of the city quietly and humbly, just as Jesus himself is quiet and humble. The people respond to the sight: it reminds them of the pomp and ceremony that Roman emperors and governors like to use in their triumphal parades. So they shout and make merry and throw down branches for this triumphant entry, but the donkey and its rider walk silently on. No one knew at the time, but this happy parade would be re-enacted every year in homage to the Lord and as a reminder to the world of its triumphant king.

In our church services, as in the Lord's life itself, this moment of simple joy and celebration is quickly overtaken by the solemn seriousness of Holy Week, by the cruel capture of the Lord and his summary execution. But here in this moment, in the simple streets of Jerusalem, the wonderful truth and the humble greatness of the Lord is seen and celebrated and gives cause for rejoicing. And a donkey, the same animal as that which featured in the humble beginnings of Christ's life in Bethlehem, features once again as his life nears its climactic moment.

Symbolic actions bring the truth home to us in a way that words never can. Seeing somebody do something impresses itself on our hearts and minds more powerfully than anything anyone might say. We are quite simply more impressed by what we see than by what we hear. When Pope Francis was first elected to be the successor of Saint Peter, his first venture outside was to go to the island of Lampedusa in the southern Mediterranean to visit the migrants who had escaped drowning in their desperate attempts to reach a better life. This action was filmed and transmitted around the globe immediately. Lampedusa was on our screens: we could not miss it or avoid it.

The Holy Father understands that these actions are powerful ways in which to promote good deeds in us all. Do it first yourself!

It is the same for us in all the actions of our lives. What we do speaks volumes. Our actions, more than any words, tell other people who we are. When Jesus comes into the city, the people begin to shout, and the word they shout is, 'Hosanna'. It means 'Saviour'. It is the recognition of one who saves, and as such it is a greeting of recognition for Jesus. In the very same way, followers of the Lord today are called to live lives of saving deeds. All our actions in life can be for salvation, to rescue people from all that would destroy them.

The daily greeting we give to one another is an act of salvation. The gentle understanding we offer to one another in all our dealings is an act of salvation. The deeds of kindness that we do are acts of salvation. On one occasion when Jesus enters the town of Jericho and again is accompanied by excited crowds of people, he meets a man named Zaccheus and prompts a conversion of heart in that man. Jesus' comment is, 'Today salvation has come to this house, because this man too is a son of Abraham' (Luke 19:9).

The disciples of the Lord remembered this day of Palm Sunday in different ways, and the four Gospel accounts tell the story with slightly different emphases. This is perfectly natural, for we all remember moments and incidents in different ways, and we retell stories in our own words. But the central theme is the same: Jesus came into the city riding on a donkey. It was the donkey's great privilege that day to carry the Lord on its back, the most precious burden it ever carried. Every donkey has its day, as the writer G. K. Chesterton put it in his poem, 'The Donkey':

> Fools! For I also had my hour;
> one far fierce hour and sweet:
> there was a shout about my ears,
> and palms before my feet.[22]

It is our great privilege also as followers of the Lord to carry Christ each day into all the streets and alleyways of our life.

'Hosanna!'

22. G K. Chesterton (1874–1936), 'The Donkey'.

Monday of Holy Week

Oil of gladness

Gospel: John 12:1-11

The house was full of the scent of the ointment.

The Glasgow Empire Theatre was often known as the 'comedian's graveyard'. Working-class people of that great city would take themselves off to the theatre to be entertained, and after a hard week's work they expected a good performance in return for their money. If the comedian was only average or poor, and especially if he was English, he could expect to have things thrown at him and to be booed off stage. But for the ones they loved, it was very heaven to be there.

As well as a good comedian, the people of Glasgow have a special love of pantomime. Three thousand people would gather at the famous theatre in the pantomime season to laugh and enjoy the show. One of the performers in that theatre, Johnnie Beattie, would say that the whole experience was good therapy for life. The warmth of the crowd towards the performers on the stage and the pure joy and laughter of the evening shared by so many were the best of tonics. No need to go to the National Health Service, said Johnnie, and no need for pills. Just give them a ticket for the pantomime! The air was thick with the sound of laughter, and the theatre itself would be fit to burst with human joy.

As we enter Holy Week, we come upon a scene that is full of human warmth and affection. Jesus makes his way to the home of Martha, Mary and Lazarus, the man he raised from the dead. The place is just a few miles from Jerusalem, yet it is a world away from all the trouble and cruel suffering that awaits Jesus there. Here, in this happy house, the friends of Jesus gather for a special meal prepared in his honour. The Lord of life is with them, and they celebrate together.

Then Mary brings in a fabulous ointment – pure nard – and anoints the feet of Jesus. It is an act of great love and affection. Nothing is too good for him. This oil is used in food, in medicine and in religious acts. Its fragrance is wonderful, and soon the whole house is filled with the aroma of this nard. Jesus and his presence fill the house, and now this fragrance, which tells of the loveliness of his life, also fills the place.

Whatever instinct prompted Mary to this action, Jesus allows it to be done to him, seeing in it the foreshadowing of his death and of the reverence that his poor body will receive when he is laid in the tomb. But before that happens, he will be taken and brutally treated, his body whipped and wounded, his person abused, his dignity as a human being trampled on. The extreme viciousness meted out to Jesus by his persecutors will hardly be recompensed even by ointment as precious and as valuable as this nard. The objection raised by Judas Iscariot about the 'wastage' that this anointing represents is both hypocritical and petty, seen against the wastage that people will soon make of the person and the body of Jesus himself.

Every day when we arise from slumber our first act is to wash and cleanse ourselves. It is good to be clean. We feel good when we are clean. It is also a kindness to others not to appear in their presence unkempt and unpleasant. When work is done and we gather with one another for a dinner or social occasion, we like to anoint ourselves with oil and so be presentable in the world.

This cleansing of our bodies needs to be replicated equally in our heart, mind and soul. To be clean of heart, to have a fragrance in our person, is the greatest way to be human in this world. If our life is fragrant, its effect will be felt all around us in the lives of other people. Just as that nard used to anoint the Lord filled the whole house with its scent, so goodness and kindness in a human soul fills the world about it.

When people die and their bodies lie still in death, we are at our most reverent towards them. Their life journey over, we acknowledge their struggles and their efforts. We honour the dead. One of the great reverences still being done to this day is the recovery of soldiers' remains from World War One, and their careful and reverent reburial in holy ground. Yet in life, our foolish ways, leading us into conflict and war, show little reverence for young lives about to be wasted.

Away from battlefields, many people's lives are scarred and wounded by the ill treatment that is meted out to them. The list of our social ills is a long one. What shall we do about it? Judas was all for selling the nard and obtaining money to give to the poor. Economic actions have their place, but Mary's action speaks louder. Love people, celebrate people and honour people. Let your every human encounter be kind. This is what the anointing with nard is telling us. When love is at work in our lives, its fragrance fills the whole house. Everyone can see. Everyone can share the scent. Nothing works like love.

Mary anointed the feet of Jesus out of love for him and out of gratitude for all that he had done for her and her family. For Jesus, it must have been a great comfort to be on the receiving end of such love. Their home was his home in this world, if only for a fleeting time. And as he thought of the coming days and the end that he so surely knew, this fragrant oil spoke to him of beauty and loveliness.

In a world of troubles, it is our great joy and privilege to be able to bring the oil of comfort and gladness into the lives of others. The Lord gives us a grace to live by and a grace to share. Let its fragrance fill the house.

> 'This I believe: I shall see the goodness of Yahweh, in the land of the living.' (Psalm 27:13)

Tuesday of Holy Week

This world's suffering

Gospel: John 13:21-33, 36-38

Night had fallen.

The Divine Comedy by Dante is a great poem, an epic that tells of the soul's journey to God. In the poem, the author himself, accompanied by the Roman poet Virgil, travels through the realms of hell, purgatory and finally heaven itself. In the first part of his journey, through the horrors of hell, Dante sees many frightful sights and some familiar faces, and is instructed about all the wickedness that is done upon the Earth. The great sins are seen in all their ugliness – lust, gluttony, greed, wrath, heresy, violence, fraud and treachery. It is in the ninth circle of hell, the deepest circle, that Dante comes upon the figure of Judas Iscariot. Poor Judas is being held in Satan's mouth, his back forever seared by Satan's claws.

In this story and this vision, Dante is expressing the traditional view of the fate of Judas, who is lost because he chose to be lost, and whose sin is regarded as the greatest sin – that of betraying Christ to his enemies. But perhaps the Lord himself has a more compassionate view.

Judas clearly lost his way. He was a man who was attracted to Jesus and whom Jesus entrusted with the office of treasurer for the group of disciples. He may well have been a political zealot, keen to see freedom for his people from the domination of Roman power. But somewhere along the line Judas began to have doubts about Jesus, whose conversations began to include references to personal suffering.

The profile of Messiah in Judas' mind and his impression of the man Jesus with whom he walked were beginning to come apart. Yet when Judas decided to hand Jesus over to the authorities – to be their man on the inside – he had no intention of seeing Jesus condemned to death. That much is very clear. So when Jesus was condemned, Judas was in torment and beside himself with grief at what he had done, at the part he had played. He, the betrayer, must have felt betrayed. Scattering the 30 pieces of silver on the Temple floor, he went off and took his own life (Matthew 27:3-10).

In the traditional understanding of these things, down through the years, suicide has been regarded as a sin, an offence against the gift of life that God gives to us. People who killed themselves were regarded as being lost forever. If life were measured simply in cold, mathematical and objective ways, then that conclusion would make sense, just as two and two make four. But life is not so simple, and our understanding of ourselves and of our souls has grown with the years, and the great social sciences of psychology and psychiatry give us insight into our torments and our struggles.

I met a lady one day in a cemetery. She was keening over a grave. Not just crying, keening. She was clearly inconsolable. Gradually and gently I learned from the lady that the person she was mourning was her son who, in his twenties with two small children and separated from their mother, was riven with torment at not seeing his children. Unable to wait for the court date that might help his situation, he was in despair and had taken his own life. The pain of this story was all too evident to me in the sight of that woman at the grave.

In the Gospel story that John writes about the last fateful evening of Christ's life, we hear how Judas goes out and, in

John's words, 'Night had fallen.' With this phrase, John captures for us the darkness of the world and the darkness of evil deeds. Jesus has told Judas to hurry, to get on with it. You can feel the nervousness in Jesus at the prospect of the trouble that is coming to him. Now that he has sent Judas out, the wheels have been set in motion. Now the action begins. Now I will be glorified, Jesus says. Now what looks like disaster will come to be seen for what it is – the love that perseveres to the end.

It is at this point that Peter makes his bold assertion that he will lay down his life for the Lord. Jesus has no time for heroics of this kind, and firmly lets Peter know that this will not happen – at least, not yet. In later days, Peter will indeed fulfil his boast and lay down his life for his Master, but by then he will no longer be a boaster. His denial of Jesus, when it happens, brings Peter to his knees. He did not know he was so weak. He did not know that an innocent question asked by a serving girl would cause him to panic. But Peter learns a great lesson.

'There is nothing I cannot master with the help of the One who gives me strength' (Philippians 4:13), but by ourselves we are very frail. This is not abject religion, but sound sense. None of us has anything to boast about to God. We are creatures of the Earth, and sometimes we are frail creatures of earth. It is good to know that. The cock crow that alerted Peter to his foolish boast and to his miserable failure is a sound for us all to listen to.

In God's grace and by God's grace we are lovely people, but when that grace is lacking, or when we are robbed of that grace by the cruelties of this world, then we are cast down. Then it is no wonder that we cry, as Peter cried, and wept his bitter tears. It is no wonder, then, that people lose heart, give up and end their own lives. It seems to them a sweet escape from the pain that is too much to bear.

For all of us, our great need is compassion, and we have come to know in Christ Jesus that God is a God of compassion, a God who suffers with us. The Lord who suffered the agony of the cross will comfort us in our agonies and bring us to share in his glory. It is for us, then, to become in our daily lives 'compassionate friends'.

'In you, Yahweh, I take shelter.' (Psalm 71:1)

Wednesday of Holy Week

Your own words

Gospel: Matthew 26:14-25

'They are your own words,' answered Jesus.

There is a great phrase that we use in Scotland whenever we wish to exonerate ourselves or to excuse ourselves from blame in any situation. We say, 'It wasnae me!' It is a very popular phrase, and a humorous comment that is made in awkward situations. 'Whoever it was, it wasnae me!' A similar comment or phrase does the rounds at the Last Supper, when Jesus drops the bombshell that somebody at the table there with him is about to betray him. This comment blows up in everyone's face and bedevils the feeling of togetherness that might have been growing as they shared a meal together. Suddenly everyone is a suspect, and a tension must have descended on the gathering.

With typical leadership – let's get to the bottom of this! – Peter tells John to lean over and ask him who the betrayer is (John 13:24). The answer Jesus gives leaves most of them no wiser. One who shares this bread with him will betray him. They all do that. Then the merry sound is heard: 'It wasnae me!' In the Gospel account it is expressed as a question: 'Not I, Lord, surely?' The words of Jesus have not only set them questioning what they have done, but also what they might be capable of doing. Judas, when his turn comes, jumps on the bandwagon sound that they all make and hides his guilt in the common sound: 'Not I, Rabbi, surely?'

The venue for the meal was arranged earlier when Jesus sent two of the disciples to 'so-and-so in the city'. I wonder who that 'so-and-so' is. Presumably it is a person Jesus already knows from earlier times in Jerusalem, a friendship or acquaintance made in quieter days. For it is clear that anyone Jesus meets would not be forgotten. The meeting would be a true human encounter of kindness, openness and growing trust. Jesus is the true human being, and every meeting would be done in grace. His every word would be kind and considered, his every gesture generous. Now Jesus needs a room for a special meal, and he can rely on Mr So-and-so to provide it. He is not disappointed.

And so they gather at table. Tables are precious places in our lives. We gather around them not just to eat, but also to be with one another in the eating, to be nourished together by sustaining food, and to enjoy each other's company. In an age of fast food and individual living, many of us do not know sufficiently the joy and the delight of table fellowship, good food and good company. In my own life, widowed as I am now more than a year, the memory of so many meals shared with Margaret, my wife, at our dining table over the years continues today to give me great joy and to sustain me in spirit.

When Jesus chooses to make public the coming fact of his betrayal, his disclosure may well have been prompted by the sheer pressure of sorrow that he is feeling over the issue. It is not easy to be in someone's company with such a hugely unspoken issue there between you. It has to be said. It needs to be voiced. And in the saying, there would be a desire in Jesus to see, even at this late hour, the chance of a change of heart in Judas. Jesus is a saviour to the very end. He is not a destroyer.

When Judas looks into the eyes of Jesus and utters the refrain, 'Not I, Rabbi, surely?' he receives the answer that he both deserves and needs for his salvation. Jesus says, 'They are your own words.' This answer should be written large for every one of us. We are responsible for every word we utter. So many words are uttered each day. How many fall to the ground unheard? Unhelpful words, perhaps. How many words wound others? How many of those words are we responsible for?

In our daily conversations, we must hold one another responsible for the things we say to each other. If we allow others to say wounding things and to get away with saying them, they will continue in the same vein. If we are not challenged about our speech, we will begin to think there is nothing wrong with what we say. We will even feel justified in giving harmful vent to anger, retaliation and jealousy, and persuade ourselves that we are only sticking up for ourselves. We will develop a self-image that tells us we are strong-minded people who call a spade a spade, when in fact we are merely angry people who think that free speech means we can say whatever we like!

Words are wonderful things when we learn how to speak them well. There is a powerful scene in one of Jennifer Worth's stories, *Call the Midwife*, on BBC television, where two very shy people meet and are attracted to one another. One is a timid nursing assistant who will not speak at all; the other a garrulous vicar who cannot stop talking. When they find the courage to confide in one another, the nurse explains that she was bullied as a child and so retreated inside herself. The vicar explains how his parents' marriage was so bitter that, as a child, he could not bear the dreadful silences, for fear of what was coming next, and so he filled the silences with his own words. Now, in meeting and recognising the kindliness in one another, they begin to speak and to speak well, without fear.

At the table on the last night of his life, Jesus is about to enter a world of suffering where the battle will be fought with many words, and he will be accused of many things. His words throughout it all are a lesson for us. Today's lesson is simple enough: 'They are your own words.'

'The Lord . . . has given me a disciple's tongue.'
(Isaiah 50:4)

Maundy Thursday

An education

Gospel: John 13:1-15

He then poured water into a basin and began to wash the disciples' feet.

I was sitting in the lecture hall of the Alphonsian Academy in Rome, struggling to understand the words of the lecturer as he spoke in the beautiful language of Italy. My Italian was incipient. Just beginning. In the course of the lecture, the professor reminded us of the great maxim about teaching and about the best form of education. He said, 'Tell me and I will forget. Show me and I will remember. Involve me and I will understand.'[23] It is a great lesson in how to drive the point home. We can see its truth quite simply.

Many lessons, many sermons, many words have flown away on the wind. They are forgotten. But tell me a story and I will most likely remember it and even be able to tell that story to another. Stories capture us – fairy stories from childhood, good novels, parables. Jesus found his preferred way of teaching through telling stories. But, as the lecturer reminded us, the best way of all to come to understanding is to be actively involved in the learning process. So, for example, the exercise of seminar work requires us to do our own research on a subject and to present it to others in the class.

And so we come to the 'last class' given by Jesus to his disciples before he suffers. Jesus has spoken with his friends

23. This is generally referred to as being a Chinese proverb.

over the three years of their journey. He has told them many stories – the great parables that have come down to us in the Gospels. Now he uses the most impressive form of education that there is – an action lesson that involves them fully. He gets down on the floor and washes their dusty feet. All his disciples, including Judas who is about to betray him, have their feet washed, and all the time they are wondering, 'What is this all about?'

Peter, of course, strong-willed man that he is, is having none of it. What Jesus is doing is completely out of order. Ridiculous, even. Nobody in their right mind does this! This is slave work, not the actions of a free man. It is dishonourable to stoop so low – dishonourable for Jesus, and dishonourable for Peter for allowing it to happen. The world as Peter understands it, and as we understand it, does not involve making yourself an unworthy slave. Peter's protest demands an explanation. How is he to get his head around this? Peter's quandary, his incomprehension, is helpful for us, for now the Lord will explain all.

The direct answer that Jesus gives to Peter is, if you do not let me wash your feet, you cannot have anything in common with me. To be part of the life of Christ Jesus we must allow the Lord to wash our feet. Then we must learn how to wash the feet of one another. There are no slaves. There are no unworthy people. How does this happen?

In the world we have ties of blood and family. We have ties of friendship and of acquaintance. We have ties of citizenship and mutual agreement. We even have ties of mutual non-aggression! After that there comes suspicion, indifference and war. In the world I can be kind, I can be generous, I can be considerate: God has made us this way. The signs of God are there if we can see them. But I can also be your enemy and come to blows with you. I never thought to go so far as to wash another's feet. What is Jesus saying to me?

It is not so much what we can do for one another; it is what we can *be* for one another. Here am I among you as one who serves, says the Lord. This is a revolution. This turns the world on its head, that I should place myself at your service. Not as a slave or a skivvy, but as the greatest way of living in the love that God has for all of us.

In telling us this story, John the Evangelist begins by saying that Jesus knows exactly who he is. He knows what power and authority he has as God's Son. He knows what lies ahead of him in terms of suffering. He is not a helpless victim of his life or his circumstances. He is a fully mature person in mind and heart, a tremendous human being. This is the man who gets down on his knees to wash feet!

What kind of lesson is this? What does it mean for my life now as a follower of the Lord? How do I relate to other people, friends or foes, now that I have witnessed this? Clearly it is not for me to go lording it over others in any way. Rather I must serve them. I must serve in everything I do from now on. I must serve the cause of right.

The first way in which I learn – before I do anything for anybody else – is by allowing the Lord to wash my feet. This must mean sitting still in the Lord's presence, as the disciples did in the upper room. Moments of silence in the Lord's presence allow the Lord to approach me, to speak to me and to refresh my soul in that encounter.

Too often in life we feel uncomfortable in letting others do a kind deed for us. Our independent lifestyle has made us strangers to acts of mutual kindness so that we are often surprised to find how kind people really are. Let others be kind to you. Let them show you their love for you. It won't hurt you.

In this experience of being kindly done to, we learn most of all how very much we belong to one another and have need of one another in this world. Out of this humble and humbling experience we will find our own way to then be servants one of another.

When we come into this world, we need others to take care of us all the time. In old age, the story will be the same. We need the service of others. In between those two stages of life we seem to forget the lesson. It is time to learn it once more.

> 'What return can I make to Yahweh for all his goodness to me?' (Psalm 116:12)

Good Friday

Jesus of Nazareth – King of the Jews

Gospel: John 18–19

I was born for this, I came into the world for this: to bear witness to the truth.

It begins in a garden and it ends in a garden. And between the two gardens is a story of atrocity. The first garden is Gethsemane, and I can claim some attachment to that place. As a child, rooting around in cupboards at home, I came across a plastic kind of button which held inside a leaf of some sort. It turned out to be a souvenir, a leaf from an olive tree from the Mount of Olives. My father, a soldier in the middle of a war, visited Gethsemane during those years when the whole world endured the passion, and this button he brought home with him. In discovering that souvenir I felt a closeness, a connection, to the Lord himself.

The great drama of Jesus' arrest takes centre stage in the court of Pontius Pilate, the Roman Governor of Judea. This military official is about to meet the greatest person he will ever know on this Earth, and during their time together, Pilate and Jesus will hold some very telling conversations. But at first Pilate is simply irritated at having his breakfast disturbed. Who is this man and what has he done? Peremptory questions are quickly followed by a directive to go away and sort it out yourselves.

When informed that his visitors are looking for the death penalty, Pilate goes inside, knowing now that he must interrogate this man. Let us establish the facts. Are you a king? Pilate is looking for surface answers. Are you dangerous or just daft? Jesus challenges him. Do you genuinely want to know about me, or simply get rid of me? This answer puts Jesus and Pilate on the same level. Man to man, you might say. Before that Pilate thought he held the higher ground.

Now Jesus can speak. And now we hear, in clear language, Jesus tell us exactly who he is. 'Yes, I am a king. I was born for this. I came into the world for this: to bear witness to the truth; and all who are on the side of truth listen to my voice.' Now we know. Pilate, the Gentile, has asked the important question on our behalf, and Jesus has shared with us the truth about himself.

At first this answer makes little impact on the hardened soldier. He does not have time to deal in little things like truth. He has to deal with law and order, security and force. As a governor he has to give some place to fairness and justice, but keeping the peace comes first, and truth is of little help in that matter. Power and persuasion are better tools for the job.

Pilate goes out to appeal to the crowd to go easy on this man. He is no threat to anyone. He tries to bargain. They shout for Barabbas. So now Pilate will try to meet them halfway. He has Jesus scourged, and this gives his soldiers the opportunity for some fun. They can use up some of their energy and annoyance on Jesus' flesh, and then have a laugh at his expense. A purple robe for kingship and a crown made from thorns. 'Hail, king of the Jews!'

It is in this foolish state, a mocked man, that Pilate now intends to parade Jesus to show to the crowd how pathetic Jesus is, how harmless, and to try and engage some sympathy for the man. We have had our fun with him. Now we can let him go. But against his calculations, the crowd, on seeing the bloodied prisoner, now bay for blood.

Pilate goes back inside. This is getting serious. He asks that lovely question, 'Where do you come from?' It is the question we all ask when we want to know someone properly. It is a deep question, a caring question. But it is too late for that now. Having given way to the crowd and tortured this man, he cannot now expect this man to calmly begin to tell him who he is. Pilate is losing his grip. The tide is running against him.

He begins to speak about power, trying to cajole an answer out of Jesus. Jesus is not affected by this ruse, but he answers kindly. It is not your fault, he tells Pilate. The people outside are the ones who have started this charade. Pilate is moved by this answer. The prisoner has expressed compassion for his judge. Pilate now wants to set him free. Irritation at being disturbed so early in the morning has become annoyance and frustration with a baying mob, and indifference to the prisoner has now become a feeling of support for this threatened man.

One more push from the crowd is all it takes now to tip the scales. They threaten Pilate himself. If you let this man go, you are no friend of Caesar. Oh, how we like to put the squeeze on people in our arguments! His back against the wall, Pilate keeps calling Jesus 'your king', trying to push the pressure back on his accusers. Surely you don't want me to crucify your king! But the crowd is ahead of him. We have no king but Caesar. Pilate is now completely cornered. He has no way out except to give them what they want and send Jesus to his death. He might wash his hands, but he will never be rid of the memory of what happened this day and of his part in it.

Could Pilate look Jesus in the eye after giving sentence? I doubt it. Not after this encounter. He is a beaten man. He must be furious with the crowd and angry with himself at what has taken place. He, the governor, has been overruled by a mob. He isn't so mighty after all. But the argument is not finished. While Jesus makes his way to Calvary and to the cross, Pilate orders a notice to be written out. It will say, 'Jesus of Nazareth, King of the Jews.' So angry is Pilate that he is determined to rub their noses in it, these people who overpowered him. Put that notice in three languages, he orders – Hebrew, Latin and Greek – and the whole world will know that this man is the king of the Jews! And when his opponents come back to complain about his action Pilate will have no more nonsense from them. *Quod scripsi, scripsi!* 'What I have written, I have written.'

When Pilate asked Jesus, 'Are you a king?' Jesus replied, 'Yes I am a king. I was born for this, I came into the world for this: to bear witness to the truth; and all who are on the side of truth listen to my voice.' Pilate now knows this to be true. He has been in the presence of a good man, a man for whom truth is important. He may not realise it, but in writing that notice Pilate, too, speaks the truth and publishes it to the world. It is his order that places the notice above the head of the dying Jesus. They are his words that will be seen by everyone who passes by that place. People have been passing by that place ever since.

The story that day ended in a garden, in a new tomb close to where Jesus was crucified. But you cannot bury the truth . . .

'Father, into your hands I commit my spirit.'
(Luke 23:46)

Holy Saturday
An empty world

Philippians 2:6-11

> *He . . . emptied himself to assume the condition of a slave, and became as men are.*

My Catholic childhood, indeed my Catholic life, has been greatly warmed by the sight of the sanctuary lamp. A gentle flame, yellow within a red vase, flickering in the semi-darkness of a church and indicating the sacramental presence of the Lord in the communion bread that is kept locked within the tabernacle. In the churches of my youth, the high altar surrounded by the area of the sanctuary was centre stage for our worship, adorned with candles and flowers and surrounded by incense. At the centre of the altar, centre of centre stage, was the tabernacle, the little house in which the Lord, in sacramental bread, abides. Covered in a cloth whose colour changed with the changing liturgical season or feast – green, purple, red, white or black – this little house was the centre of the world. 'Here God lives among men.'

On Holy Saturday this little house stands open, empty and bare. No coloured covering on the tabernacle, no flowers, no candles, no sanctuary lamp burning. The Lord has been led away captive and he has been cruelly done to death. They have laid his body in a tomb in a garden close by, and now the world is empty. The Lord, whose presence has graced the Earth and whose love has filled so many hearts, is gone, crucified, dead and buried.

On this day I have always felt the absence of God from this world. I have felt completely alone. Like the day my father died. I was 41 years of age and my father had been a constant and faithful presence in my life. Now he was gone from this life, and I stood before the huge plate glass window in the office of our local undertaker and I looked out on familiar streets in my so familiar town, and I did not know this world. I felt completely alone.

When my beloved wife died and was laid in her coffin, I stood beside her and I prayed my sorrowing prayers and psalms. I looked upon her body lying there so still and I said, 'You are not here. You are gone from me.' When you lose the ones you love, there comes a sorrow you have never known before.

This is the sorrow of this day, Holy Saturday. The world is left to itself, bereft of the Lord who gives us life. And yet it must be so. Jesus became one like us in all things. Born into this world and laid in a manger. Lived in this world with nowhere to lay his head. Taken from this world in a cruel manner and laid upon a cross. Taken from the cross and laid finally in a tomb.

The silence now of that tomb and its darkness seem to spell the end of all things. Today's sorrow is like the sorrow we feel when a funeral is over. The grave is filled in and covered over. The mourners disperse to their homes. We are left with only memories and a broken heart. Things will ease, we are told, given time. But we do not need to hear that now. This is no time for consolation. Our loved one has died. There is no more to be said.

Sitting in an empty church on this day we can think of all the people whose heads are bowed in sorrow: people who really feel that death is the end of all things; people who mourn for the end of their dreams, for the end of a relationship, for the end of their own life's purpose, and for the end of life itself. Does death have the final word? Is our life ultimately a journey that goes nowhere? Do we flicker momentarily upon the stage and then are gone? Is love not stronger than this?

The garden where Jesus' body lies is a place where we should sit still on this day and think again about all the things that constitute our life. For we know something never known before. We have heard a news never heard before. This place, this garden of death, is soon to be the garden of resurrection. What happened here has forever changed the meaning of our life. What we so earnestly wish for, hope for and dream of has happened. 'Life with death contended. Combat strangely ended. Life's own champion slain, yet lives to reign.'[24]

My wife died more than a year ago and I feel her presence close beside me always. I talk to her as surely as I talk to the Lord himself. For Margaret lives with the Lord of life, as do all who have died in the Lord. Heaven is close beside us. We are surrounded by life in the Lord.

The Old Testament prophet Hosea speaks eloquently about our life and our troubles, and about the life that will be restored to us. Hear what he says:

> Come, let us return to Yahweh. He has torn us to pieces, but he will heal us; he has struck us down, but he will bandage our wounds; after a day or two he will bring us back to life, on the third day he will raise us and we shall live in his presence.
>
> *Hosea 6:1-2*

24. Easter Sequence, *Victimae paschali laudes.*

One of the great receivers of life when Christ Jesus rose from the dead was the Apostle Peter. In later years, when Peter had fully absorbed the story of the Lord's life and the story of his own, he set down in writing some thoughts for us to benefit from. He says:

> Remember, the ransom that was paid to free you from the useless way of life your ancestors handed down was not paid in anything corruptible, neither in silver nor gold, but in the precious blood of a lamb without spot or stain, namely Christ.
>
> *1 Peter 1:18-19*

Yes, we have been set free from useless living, from foolishness and from folly. Jesus, rising from the darkness, sets us free. In this silence of the garden tomb today, let us thank the Lord of life for life itself, for freedom from sin and for the promised joys and the life of the world to come.

> 'Every tongue should acclaim Jesus Christ as Lord to the glory of God the Father.' (Philippians 2:11)

Holy Saturday

Silent garden tomb

They laid him in the grave, in a tomb.
The body of the Lord so sorely used
received now by the Earth into its womb,
beloved in death, a man so much abused.

He came unto his own, who did not know
the things they did, and so they were excused.
The Lord they nailed and nailed so long ago;
we're nailing still when others are ill-used.

His mother, Mary, stood beneath the cross
and bravely watched her son so badly bruised.
Her heart was riven in two; such was her loss.
Her sorrow with her only son's confused.

The young disciple, John, stood at her side.
He saw it all which later he wrote down.
He saw the nails; he saw the opened side;
he saw the lance; he saw the thorny crown.

The soldier who was on patrol that day,
in charge of the deployment at the scene,
was heard to utter amazement and to say,
'This man was surely great,' no might have been.

They carried his dear body to the place,
a garden tomb in which no man had lain.
In clothes they shrouded him, and o'er his face
another cloth, all covering the pain.

And spices too they brought to honour him.
Sweet fragrance of a life the sweetest, best.
A stone to close the entrance and within
the darkness of our death, our greatest test.

The spirit of the Lord has left this world
to wander for a while among the dead,
to greet the faithful, a promise to unfurl
to gather them around, the grateful dead.

My thoughts now turn to loved ones who are gone:
my mother, father, ancestors and all
who lived their lives so bravely every one
and hoped to hear at last the faithful call.

I think as well about my own dear wife,
my Margaret who left this world so dear;
the girl who ended for me all my strife
and took away confusion and all fear.

Her body lies along in holy ground.
I visit that dear plot so faithfully,
and I pray the rosary and lift the sound
and remember all my loved ones constantly.

And now my thoughts go on to other fields
where brave young men from all sides met their doom
in wars we fought so futilely, there bleeds
the memory, the millions and the gloom.

If we will learn a truth, then let it be
that crucifying innocents is done.
This cannot be the way to set us free –
the bullet and the bayonet and the gun.

Come back again and in the garden stay
beside the tomb of one they crucified.
In silence let us kneel and softly pray
for grace to love and follow one who died.

Brian Fahy

Easter Day
Roll away the stone

Gospel: Matthew 28:1-10; Mark 16:1-7; Luke 24:1-12; John 20:1-9

Who will roll away the stone for us?

In 1974 a glam-rock band, Mott the Hoople, came out with a very popular song entitled *Roll Away the Stone*. It has a very catchy tune, it was a fun song, and it told the usual story of boy meets girl and loses her and wins her back. The title of the song implies the resurrection of the relationship after their boy/girl troubles. For me, a young priest in south London at that time, the title of the song immediately put me in mind of Easter Day and the most amazing discovery ever made by humankind, when some women walked to a tomb, wondering among themselves who was going to roll away the stone from the entrance to the tomb, to allow them to complete the anointing of the dead body of the Lord.

After the horrors of Good Friday and the silence of Saturday, the women in Jesus' group of followers set out in the early morning to complete the anointing of the body that they only half did on that Friday evening. It must be a silent group that sets out that morning, just as the sun is rising, lost in their own thoughts about what has happened to their Lord. But they do talk among themselves and their big question is, 'Who will roll away the stone for us from the entrance to the tomb?'

When they arrive at the tomb their question is already answered. The stone, large as it is, is already rolled away, and the tomb is empty. No body. No Lord. But there is a young man there in a white robe, who explains what has happened. Why look among the dead for someone who is alive? The Lord is risen, he says. No one is expecting this. But the women look and they see the linen cloths that bound his body – the very cloths they wrapped him in. The cloths are there, but there is no body. Now go and tell the disciples!

Not only is there no body; there are no guards either! We are told that they have left the tomb and reported some kind of convulsion or earthquake and the stone rolling away. And no body. Under instructions from the authorities these guards will say that the disciples came and stole the body. Not likely, when an armed guard is in place, but it will do. And so that is the story that is spread abroad.

Now Peter and John come running and they go right inside the tomb. A thorough investigation is needed, and Peter is just the man for it. He sees the cloths and then he sees the face covering. And no body. And then he remembers all the things that Jesus said and which he could not fathom before. He fathoms them now! He must rise from the dead. What could that possibly mean? Now Peter knows.

As those two disciples make their dizzy way back to the upper room, Mary of Magdala stays behind, weeping in the garden. A man approaches and asks her the reason for her tears. Maybe he knows where the body is. Then he speaks her name, and she would recognise this voice anywhere. How often has she listened to him speaking wonderful things! She looks up through her tears and she sees him.

Now the sightings begin in earnest. The disciples gathered in the upper room see him. He appears to Peter. Two disciples on their way to a village meet him. They all see him. You are my witnesses, Jesus tells them. Now you must go out to the whole world and tell this good news. Death is defeated. Sin is ended. Love is alive. The stone is rolled away.

The arguments that have gone on since that Easter Day against this good news say that the disciples stole the body and pretended the resurrection. Would shocked and distressed men, people shattered to the core, even want to consider such a ruse. To devote their lives to a lie? To do so in the name of goodness? And be prepared to die for that lie? I think not.

We stake our lives on good things, not on follies. Human joy cannot be faked. People cannot be truly happy unless they are truly happy! When Jesus ascended to heaven, the disciples went back into Jerusalem – the city of their greatest terror – absolutely rejoicing. The Lord is alive and the Lord is with them. And this indeed becomes a great Christian greeting. 'The Lord be with you!'

Yes, the tomb is empty. Death and the deeds of darkness have done their utmost and they lie defeated. There is no sorrow that will not be overcome. The tomb is empty and the world is filled with the light of the Lord. There is no need for alarm. No need to fear. Come sorrow, come sadness. Come wicked deeds, come woe. Come sudden death, come lingering days. Do not be afraid. I am with you always. I have overcome the world.

The 1974 song of Mott the Hoople tells of people who would mock the love story, saying that the young lovers are doomed to sadness, but the singer believes in the triumph of love. *Roll Away the Stone* is resurrection music. For all the sorrows of this life, from broken hearts to broken bodies and broken lives, the Lord shines the light of his risen life upon us. We shall not be left in the tomb to die. The stone is rolled away.

As the sun rises, so the Lord shines on my life today. He tells us to make our way to Galilee, the place of our true home. Let us come home to ourselves and let the Lord show his face to us.

'I shall not die, I shall live.' (Psalm 118:17)